How to Start a Home-Based
Antiques Business

Help Us Keep This Guide Up to Date

Every effort has been made by the author and editors to make this guide as accurate and useful as possible. However, many things can change after a guide is published—establishments close, phone numbers change, facilities come under new management, etc.

We would love to hear from you concerning your experiences with this guide and how you feel it could be made better and be kept up to date. While we may not be able to respond to all comments and suggestions, we'll take them to heart and we'll make certain to share them with the author. Please send your comments and suggestions to the following address:

The Globe Pequot Press
Reader Response/Editorial Department
246 Goose Lane
P.O. Box 480
Guilford, CT 06437

Or you may e-mail us at:
editorial@GlobePequot.com

Thanks for your input.

HOME-BASED BUSINESS SERIES

How to Start a Home-Based
Antiques Business

Fourth Edition

Jacquelyn Peake

revised and updated by Bob Brooke

The
Globe
Pequot
Press

GUILFORD, CONNECTICUT

To buy books in quantity for corporate use
or incentives, call **(800) 962–0973, ext. 4551,**
or e-mail **premiums@GlobePequot.com.**

Cover photos: Clockwise from top left: Eric Kamp/Index Stock; © Photodisc; Eye Wire
Cover design: Nancy Freeborn
Text design: Mary Ballachino

ISSN 1552-728X
ISBN 0-7627-3445-0

Manufactured in the United States of America
Fourth Edition/First Printing

Contents

Contents

Contents

Introduction

Running an antiques shop from your home will be fun and rewarding, in more ways than you can imagine right now. You'll make a few mistakes along the line. Fortunately, those you do make will undoubtedly be small ones. After all, you're not going to be responsible for warehouses full of antiques or budgets the size of the national debt. Your contact with the public will be low-key and pleasant. The biggest error you're likely to make will be in occasionally buying stock you can't sell at your usual markup.

In Chapter 2 you'll learn about two government-sponsored sources where you can get practical, down-to-earth information on managing your business. The extensive information you'll gain from their counselors is actually free. Chapter 2 will also show you how and where to apply for any necessary permits and how to choose and record your shop's name. It will give you guidelines on ways to adapt your home to accommodate your shop and will help you estimate the costs of remodeling. This chapter will also help you understand the advantages and disadvantages of working with a partner.

Unless you've owned a business before, you may not understand the reason for constructing a business plan. Chapter 3 will explain the reasons, then walk you through the process. You'll find a completed hypothetical business plan to follow as you design your own.

Admittedly, most of us don't enjoy keeping detailed records, but therein lies the key to success in this or any other business. Chapter 4 will help you understand which records you need to keep and how to go about the process. You'll find some suggestions on specific forms that can make record keeping quite simple.

Chapter 5 is devoted to creative ways to keep your shop well stocked with salable antiques. You'll learn how to know, in advance, what your potential customers will buy. You'll find descriptions of the places where most antiques dealers acquire their merchandise. This chapter also describes several nonantique items you might carry that can mean extra cash for you.

Chapter 6 shows how you can increase your business and income by buying and selling antiques on the Internet. You'll find information for both new and experienced Internet users.

Knowing which antiques to buy is one thing. Pricing them to make a profit is quite another. In Chapter 7 you'll discover the realities of overhead and how it affects your pricing structure. You'll see how the services you offer have a direct bearing on your markup. Since none of us is perfect, you're bound occasionally to buy antiques you simply can't sell at your usual markup. This chapter shows you a few ways to move those antiques and recoup your investment.

Buying salable antiques and pricing them well are the first steps toward selling them. Chapter 8 describes how you can then *display* your antiques to the greatest advantage, including the importance of correct lighting.

With all of the above in place, you still have to let people know you're in business. That's where Chapter 9 comes into play. It shows several creative ways to market your business to the public, including traditional advertising methods and less well known but even more effective public relations techniques.

Finally, Chapter 10 describes several additional ways you can use your knowledge of antiques to create extra income. You'll learn the nitty-gritty of selling at antiques shows, for example. You'll also discover how to expand your capabilities by holding estate sales and appraising antiques for others.

You should read the entire book *at least once and preferably twice* before you make any move toward starting your home-based business. Some topics are treated in two or more chapters, and you need to get the whole picture before making any important decisions.

So read the book through, then go back and read each chapter separately as you discover you need information on specific subjects. What could be more satisfying than being self-employed and working with the antiques you love? Welcome aboard!

Chapter One

So You Want to Own an Antiques Shop

M ost people become antiques dealers rather innocently. More often than not, their road to becoming their own boss begins at local yard or garage sales where they buy items that they like for their home. Eventually, they find themselves buying similar items and thus begin a collection. This collection leads to exposure to other items and that leads to another collection and, eventually, another. By now their house is so full that in order to continue collecting, they resort to selling some of the pieces that perhaps aren't as good at their own yard or garage sale.

While yard and garage sales are where many antiques and collectibles enter the market, prices can be limited here because everyone is looking for a bargain. So ambitious wannabee dealers seek out flea markets where they can not only sell their items for higher prices but are also exposed to collectors seeking those items. Thus begins the route to becoming an antiques dealer.

Almost all dealers start out selling antiques part-time. Some of them use this as a sideline business to supplement their regular job. Others see it as a profitable hobby, a way to have the fun of working with antiques and make a little money on the side. A few dealers started out buying and selling antiques simply because their own collections were about to run them out of the house. That's exactly the way one dealer got into the business. His tiny home could have been a museum of fine Oriental pottery. Bowls, urns, and plates covered every horizontal surface from the coffee table to the refrigerator. The walls bristled with shelves holding even more pottery. So, he started selling off the less desirable pieces. Of course, that just gave him money to buy *more* pottery. Since he had the knack of finding fine pottery everywhere he went, he never really solved the problem of an overcrowded house, but he did make quite a lot of money.

What nearly always happens with these part-time dealers is that after a year or more, they begin to feel confident about their ability to spot good buys that they know will sell. They learn the types of antiques that people in their area are looking for, and they learn how to buy at prices that will practically guarantee money in their pockets.

Finally, they become so addicted—dealing in antiques can be an incurable addiction—that they begin toying with the idea of fulfilling the American Dream—owning their own business. In this case, it would be an antiques shop. For whatever reason, though, many of them don't want to open a shop in a commercial building. That's when they start looking into the possibility of owning a home-based antiques shop.

You wouldn't be reading this book if you didn't have such a thought in the back of your mind. You may have a fairly decent job now but are looking for one by which you can make a living without having to put up with a demanding boss. You may be retired (or close to it) and casting about for a profession in which you can supplement your retirement income and keep active in the community. You may be a homemaker who needs to add to the family income but who doesn't want to be away from home for most of the day. All of these are legitimate reasons for considering a home-based antiques shop. Should you decide to go ahead with such a shop, you'll be one of a growing number of men and women who are discovering the advantages of working from their home.

Before you call the painter in to make a sign for your front yard, though, you need to sit yourself down and do some honest soul-searching. The decision to run an antiques shop from your home is not one you make some morning before you've had your coffee. Not everyone is cut out for this type of self-employment, in spite of how enticing it may sound.

Ideally, you'll be a high-energy person who takes personal responsibility for your own actions. You'll enjoy competition and have a fine sense of your own worth. You like people and people like you. You enjoy working and expect to be rewarded well for your efforts.

Read on to learn some of the pros and cons of the business.

Disadvantages of Owning a
Home-Based Antiques Shop

Like most of us, you've probably worked at a *regular* job sometime in your life. In spite of having to put up with all its attendant problems, you did have a regular paycheck, maybe health benefits, paid vacations, and probably some job security.

You'll have none of that when you're self-employed as the owner of a home-based antiques shop. Here are some disadvantages:

- Your only paycheck is the profit from your sales, and that will fluctuate with the seasons—boom and bust. You'll probably have months when sales are very high (spring until the winter holidays, as a rule) and others (typically, January and February) when you'll twiddle your thumbs half the time, wondering if anyone will ever come in the door again.

- You'll have to pay for your own health insurance, and, because of your status as a self-employed person, your social security contributions to the government will be doubled.

- If you want to take a vacation, you'll have to either close the shop or hire someone to run it for you in your absence.

- You can also forget the forty-hour workweek. Even if you keep your shop open only eight hours a day five days a week, you'll spend many additional hours acquiring stock and doing book work.

- Since you'll be working out of your home, many people won't think you're really working. Friends will drop by, expecting you to sit and share a cup of tea with them. Some of them may call you on your business phone just to chat.

- Customers won't respect your posted hours, either. One owner of an in-home antiques shop had people banging on his shop door at 10:00 P.M. because they knew he was at home upstairs!

- Unless you have another source of income (or your spouse is bringing home a paycheck), opening a shop is highly risky for anyone with dependents. It may be many months before you show a profit.

- Since you'll be working at home, you'll never be able to get away from work (a genuine problem for workaholics). Unless you have more willpower than most people, you'll manage to wander back into the shop area almost every night after closing, every Sunday, even on holidays, to take care of some little detail.
- Unless you hire an assistant, you'll be working alone, and the sense of isolation can become genuinely distressing. You won't have the companionship of fellow workers or the fun of office parties.
- If you decide, for whatever reason, to close your business, you may lose all your investment and have to remove any remodeling you did to your home.

But there are many advantages.

Advantages of Owning a Home-Based Antiques Shop

Perhaps you, like many of us, became fed up working within the corporate bureaucracy or, even worse, the government. You realized that no matter how hard you worked, you'd always be a small frog in a big pond. Your strings would always be pulled by someone who had more clout than you could ever hope to have. Or maybe you're a person who wants to be in the business world, perhaps for the first time, but who likes a slower lifestyle than the one offered by the average job. You're looking for something just a little more—dare I use the word *genteel?* Or maybe you're one of those people who's always dreamed of owning your own antiques shop, and you've decided now's the time to do it. You're willing to take a few risks to make it happen.

Do I hear you shouting, "That's me! That's me!"? If so, then you're a perfect candidate for self-employment as the owner of a home-based antiques shop. Consider these advantages:

- The sense of pride and accomplishment you'll feel when you see that sign go up outside with *your* shop's name on it is hard to describe. "This is mine! I created it! I made it happen!" comes close.

- As the owner of your own shop, you'll be totally in control of your business. If you want to open your doors earlier and stay open later than your competition, you can do so. Open on Monday? Close on Monday? It's up to you. Decorate your windows with cheery checked curtains or elegant lace panels? Whatever suits you best. You'll have the freedom to make all the decisions yourself about how the business is run.

- Your commuting time and expenses will drop to zero, since you won't have to go any farther than from the back of the house to the front. If your former workplace was thirty minutes from your home, you'll save a full five hours a week in commuting time, and you won't spend many dollars each week for gasoline or transit fares.

- You'll probably be able to dress in a more casual style than allowed in most offices, thereby saving hundreds of dollars every year on clothing.

- As the owner of a business, you'll garner prestige among other businesspeople in your community, and your friends will admire your spunk. You'll have the opportunity to join the chamber of commerce and service clubs. Your network of friends will double, triple, or even quadruple, within months of opening your shop.

- The tax advantages of operating a home-based shop are numerous. You'll make one mortgage or rent payment, pay one utility bill, and you can take a large portion of those bills off your income tax as legitimate business deductions. (Your CPA will explain just what will and what won't pass muster with the IRS.)

- Since you'll be running the shop from your home, your operating expenses will be less than those of a dealer who rents commercial space, yet your markup ratio can be the same as that dealer's, meaning that you'll make more profit per sale than he or she will. If you wish, you can sell your antiques at prices lower than those of the "downtown" dealers, thereby developing a reputation among regular customers for offering quality at low prices. Yet you'll *still* make an excellent profit.

- Although these profits may be slim at first (until you've recouped your start-up costs), you have the potential for an excellent income. Everything depends on your initiative and how hard you're willing to work.

Do Some Preliminary Research

Now let's assume that, after reading the preceding pages, you're still gung ho to open your own antiques shop. Your first step will be to research the demographics of your town and then take an informal survey of the existing antiques shops to determine whether they're successful or not.

Pay a visit to your local chamber of commerce. Someone there will have a bulging file that can give you virtually all the demographic data you need. You want to check on the following:

- *What is the median income level of the town?* People buy antiques for their homes with discretionary income, after they've paid their rent and bought their groceries. These customers must have some extra cash to spend on luxuries. It's important, therefore, that there be a solid base of people in town with comfortable incomes.
- *What is the growth potential of the area?* Are companies moving to town, bringing with them jobs and additional spendable cash? Can young people find employment? Since opening a shop is a long-term proposition, it's important that the prognosis for a town's economic future be one of health and growth.
- *What is the turnover rate of shops in town?* Do most businesspeople stay in business for many years, or is there a constant opening and closing of different enterprises?
- *What is the traffic count in front of your home and on nearby arteries?* A large part of your business will come from people who see your home/shop as they commute to work or drive by on their way to somewhere else. If your chamber of commerce doesn't have these figures, go to the highway department in your city or county.

Once you're satisfied that your town has a bright future for business in general, you need to check out the future for the antiques business itself. Almost every town of any size in this country has at least one antiques shop, whether in commercial space or in a home. It's a given in this business that any well-run antiques shop will succeed if others in the general area are successful, too. Most people don't patronize only one antiques shop. If they're shopping for a specific antique (or just browsing), they'll cruise through every shop in town.

If there are no existing antiques shops, you should ask yourself, "Why not?" Maybe the population base is too small to support a shop, or perhaps most people are more interested in sports and recreation than collecting or investing in antiques.

With any kind of luck at all, though, you live in a town where many of the residents genuinely enjoy antiques. One way you can determine the success of existing shops (which would imply success in your shop) is simply to stand on the sidewalk in front of a few of them and check the number of customers going in and out. Watch especially to see how many customers come out with bags in their hands. This is pretty good evidence that they bought something.

You can also stroll inside an antiques shop on an average weekend day and watch the action on the selling floor. How many sales does the owner make in an hour? Try to figure out how much customers spent in that hour. A little quick calculation can then tell you how much the owner is taking in per day.

Most owners of antiques shops are friendly people who don't mind at all helping others, so don't hesitate to simply ask a shop owner if he is making a reasonable profit. If the shop has been there, under the same owner, for at least a year, you can be sure that person is making money. No one continues pouring funds into a losing business for more than a year.

Okay so far? Now go a bit further and ask yourself two important questions: (1) Is my home *suitable* for a home-based shop? and (2) Am *I* cut out to manage one? To help you answer these questions, take a few minutes to complete the following self-surveys. After each question you'll find space to check off an answer. (I know you were taught in school never to write in a book, but this is different. Trust me—you *should* write in this book.) Before each question I've included some information that explains the reason for the question. Each question, incidentally, relates to subjects that are covered in later chapters of this book.

Is Your Home Suitable for a Home-Based Antiques Shop?

Real estate salespeople have a formula they use to help determine the selling value of a piece of property. It's *location, location, location.* Location is vitally important to the success of a home-based antiques shop too.

Look at your home objectively, both from a customer's point of view and as a commercial establishment, and complete the following site evaluation. A quick glance down the columns will tell you whether you should go ahead with your plans to use your home for your shop.

1. Since customers will be coming to your home instead of to a commercial building, it should be easily accessible to them. You don't have to be right in the center of town, certainly, but you should have good access by automobile. The most successful businesses are those located on or near major traffic arteries. Customers will drive a few blocks out of their way to reach a shop, but most will not travel much farther than that.

   Question: Is your home located in a neighborhood where customers can find you easily? Is it situated near a major artery where there is reasonable traffic flow to create drive-by interest in the shop?

   Yes _____   No _____

2. Most of your customers will drive to your home, but parking is forbidden or highly restricted in some neighborhoods.

   Question: Will your customers be able to park at the curb in front of your home/shop or within a few blocks?

   Yes _____   No _____

3. For many weeks in winter, your shop will be open after dark. Some people are hesitant to park their car on a street that is not well lighted.

   Question: Does your street have adequate overhead lighting that illuminates it and the entrance to your shop on late afternoons in winter?

   Yes _____   No _____

4. There's nothing wrong with starting out in a small front room. But as your business grows, you will need more display space.

   Question: Is the layout of your home such that you can either remodel it to include more display space in the future or add another wing or room?

   Yes_____   No_____

5. Unless the owner of a home-based business lives alone, he must consider the needs and feelings of other family members. In most cases the space used for a home-based antiques shop usurps a living room, dining room, or some other area that was once used by the family. Understandably, they may feel a little put out if that room or rooms suddenly become filled with antiques and customers and the family is relegated to the back of the house.

No one should even consider turning part of a home into a shop if it's going to cause real dissension in the family. It's just not worth it.

Question: Does your home have a family room or some other space where everyone can gather for games, television, conversation, and entertaining friends?
Yes_____   No_____

Are You the Right Person for This Venture?

Many of us have a blind spot or two regarding our own faults and qualities, so you might photocopy these questions and ask a close friend or your spouse to evaluate you based on his own judgment of your entrepreneurial abilities.

1. A home-based antiques shop is still an antiques shop, not a hobby. It's little different from one in commercial space as far as its day-to-day operation is concerned. Barring genuine emergencies, the doors must be open regular hours on specific days. In most cases this means that you, as the owner/manager, must be there to greet customers during those hours and on those days. Certainly, you can hire part-time help (more about that later), but the main burden of running the shop will be on you.

   One home-based antiques shop owner had hung a rather crudely painted sign out front. It informed potential customers OPEN WHENEVER I'M HOME. CALL FIRST—555-3485. Guess how many customers took the time to call first and set an appointment to browse through her antiques? Not many.

   So even though maintaining your shop in your home can be far more pleasant than working eight to five for someone else, it's still a full-time job.

Question: Are you looking upon managing a home-based antiques shop as a full-time job (instead of a profitable hobby)?

Yes_____   No_____

2. Loving antiques isn't enough to ensure a profit in your shop. You must be a good businessperson too. This means understanding how to keep good records, what the relationship of profit to expense is, ways to control inventory, how much to allocate to advertising, how to establish good public relations in the community, and much more.

    Question: Have you ever worked in a business in which you were responsible for or had exposure to the behind-the-scenes side to retail selling?

    Yes_____   No_____

    If the answer to the above question is no, would you be willing to get practical experience or training before you open your shop?

    Yes_____   No_____

3. Most financial advisers suggest that anyone planning a home-based business have enough cash on hand or readily available to pay for the necessary remodeling and to buy the initial stock without having to obtain a bank loan. The reason is simple: It often takes months for a new business to begin showing a profit, yet lenders expect loan payments to come in on time every month, whether or not the shop is making money.

    Question: Do you have enough cash on hand or readily available to take care of the inevitable remodeling and opening expenses of your antiques shop?

    Yes_____   No_____

4. Most people consider self-employment because they want to be free of the corporate bureaucracy, want to have the opportunity to make as much money as their intelligence allows, and want to make their own decisions. They are independent thinkers. These people often come up with creative ideas, solutions to problems. They're self-starters who can get out of bed in the morning and begin work even though there's no time clock to punch or no supervisor to please. They stick with a project until it's finished. They're reasonably well organized and get a sense of accomplishment from a job well done. These people have usu-

ally served as officers or on committees at their churches or synagogues, in clubs, or at their children's schools.

Question: Do you consider yourself a self-starter, creative, and independent?
Yes_____   No_____

5. Only someone who genuinely loves antiques will be able to sell them with enthusiasm. That means all antiques, too, even those whose style may not be exactly to your liking. You may not be overly fond of Mission Oak, for example, yet Mission Oak is very popular right now and bringing high prices.

   A middle-aged man recently moved from Philadelphia to a small town west of St. Louis, bringing with him pieces of top-quality Chippendale and Queen Anne furniture, the type he preferred. Looking ahead to opening an antiques shop in his new home, he scouted the antiques shops and malls in the area, checking out their stock, prices, and so on. Since he had moved into an area of small towns where most people wanted late-nineteenth-century oak and primitives, that's what he noticed in the shops. He hadn't realized that his Eastern tastes may not be the same as those of the Midwest. If he did open a shop, he'd have to sell oak and primitives, among other things, or his business would fail.

   Question: Do you love and appreciate antiques enough to be able to sell any and all of them with enthusiasm?
   Yes_____   No_____

6. As with many other aspects of life—skirt lengths, architecture, music, even pets—trends in antiques change from time to time. Savvy dealers keep up with these trends.

   Remember when everyone was collecting insulators? Dealers scoured the countryside, buying all they could find for their shops. Prices went through the roof, and these dealers sold the insulators for top dollar, but that trend passed and others took its place.

   Signed aluminumware, for example, has become a legitimate collectible. Dealers and collectors are searching for aluminum trays, bowls, and novelty items of the thirties and forties, things they would have previously ignored.

   To be successful as a dealer in antiques, you must keep up with such trends, on both a national and a local level. If there appears to be a surge in interest in some period or item, then you know to begin stocking it. You can keep up with trends by reading several of the excellent trade journals and books published for dealers in antiques, such as *Antique Week, Maine Antiques Digest,* and *Southeastern Antiques and Collectibles Magazine.* Some newspapers print syndicated columns devoted to antiques. A few national magazines, such as *Forbes,* have regular departments for antiques and collectibles. By reading these publications regularly, you can keep up with what people are buying, as well as current selling prices. This information is available to you no matter where you live.

Keep up with what the decorating and home service magazines are featuring too. Over and over, new homeowners will come into your shop carrying the current issue of *Country Living, Better Homes and Gardens, Southern Living,* or some other magazine. They'll point to an illustration of a piece of furniture or decorative item and ask, "Do you have one of these?" If you have it, you've made an immediate sale.

You can tell when a trend is fading by reading the "For Sale" and auction ads in the major antiques trade papers. If many dealers and private collectors start selling off their stock in a certain category, you can be pretty sure the trend has peaked and prices will fall substantially.

Question: Will you be willing to devote several hours a week to studying antiques, their trends, and current prices?

Yes_____   No_____

7. Of course, you'll have the companionship of your customers. You will become good friends with many of them, and their visits will be bright spots in your workday. Inevitably, however, you'll spend many hours alone in your shop. Can you handle this without becoming depressed?

Question: Can you work alone without being lonely?

Yes_____   No_____

8. Good health and energy are prime attributes of the successful entrepreneur. Some people seem to be blessed with this health and energy. Others have to work at it. Regardless, it's impossible to run a business successfully if you're listless and tired all the time.

You don't have to follow the regimen of an Olympic athlete to maintain good health. All it usually takes is a sensible lifestyle. Most doctors and physical therapists today recommend no smoking, moderate or no alcohol consumption, normal weight, a low-fat, high-fiber diet, and a half hour or so every day of some kind of exercise—an early-morning brisk walk or late-afternoon workout at a gym will do wonders for your energy level.

Question: Will you make an effort to maintain a healthy lifestyle so that you'll have the energy necessary to run your business?

Yes_____   No_____

These lists can create a bit of soul-searching, and there really are no right or wrong answers to any of the questions. But your *overall* answers will show whether owning a home-based shop is practical. Go back and look at your check marks. One or two *no*'s aren't critical, so if you can answer *yes* to most of the questions, then you, too, should be able to open an antiques shop in your home with confidence.

Like any other business, the antiques business thrives when the economy is good. Despite a few recessions in the past couple of decades, the general profile of the antiques business is up. People continue to purchase antiques for pleasure and for investment. Knowledgeable people, in fact, have always invested in quality antiques for their homes. Go into the homes of affluent families today and you'll find at least a few antiques. These people realize that antiques, like real estate and fine art, are excellent investments.

The beauty of this business and for you as the owner of a home-based shop, however, is that today people don't have to be wealthy to buy antiques and collectibles for their homes. Thousands of shop owners across the country cater to middle-income Americans. They fill their shops with lovely furniture, prints, tableware, stained glass, and an infinite variety of memorabilia, all at affordable prices.

Get Experience Before You Hang Out Your Shingle

Simply loving antiques or dealing in them part-time is fun, but making the transition to full-time dealing requires some preparation.

Almost every profession requires some kind of education or training. The antiques business is no different. You certainly don't need a degree in business management, but you do need to know the basics of retail merchandising and record keeping.

What's the best way to learn the ropes? Reading this book is a good start: It contains just about everything you need to know *that can be put in a book.* Unless you have some hands-on experience in selling antiques on a day-to-day basis, however, you might be letting yourself in for some problems.

We'll assume that you really do love antiques but have never owned a shop of your own with the full responsibility of management. You can get that training in several ways:

- *Get a job in a good local antiques shop,* then use your eyes and ears to absorb every bit of knowledge you can from the owner or manager. This way, you'll see how he manages inventory, works with customers, handles difficult situations, and so forth.
- *Work in an antiques mall.* Large antiques malls sometimes hire several people to assist in selling and bookkeeping, to help customers find specific items, to watch for shoplifters, and so forth. While this is often only part-time—three or four days a week—they're getting top-notch training in the antiques business.
- *Rent space in an antiques mall.* Though you wouldn't have the responsibility of managing the entire mall, you would learn how to manage your own booth and stock. You'd also learn the best ways to display your antiques, how to shift them around to create interest, how to decorate, and how to price them realistically. In addition, you'd learn about profit margins and what people in your area are buying. At the same time, you'd be building up inventory that you can move to your own shop when you open it.
- *Join an antiques co-op.* If an antiques co-op is already in operation near your home, you could approach the owners and ask about joining it. In a co-op several dealers actually own the business jointly and usually have equal floor space in the shop. They share the responsibility of keeping the shop open, cleaning it, and so forth. They also share all expenses: rent, utilities, advertising, and so forth. This is about the only way you can actually own an antiques shop without having the entire responsibility of management.

Business School Can Help Too

To further your business knowledge, you might want to enroll in a basic business management course in the community education division of a local college or university. Seriously look at your business skills and find courses that will help you improve them. A course in how to start or run a small business would be excellent for starters. As you get into your new business, you may also want to enroll in basic record keeping, accounting, and tax courses.

Chapter Two

Getting Started

All right, so you've decided to take the plunge. You're going to become the proud owner of the best antiques shop in town. Great! Before you put out the welcome mat for that first customer, however, you need to get some advice.

Free Advice from Professionals

Free services are invaluable for anyone who's never managed a business before. What can you expect from a meeting with volunteers? Hours and hours of one-on-one consultation! The helpful people at your local or regional Small Business Development Center (SBDC) will even meet with you regularly *after* you open your shop to help guide you toward success. These centers also offer short courses on running a business, such as Understanding Financial Statements, Changing Careers, Basic Bookkeeping, Advanced Bookkeeping, and Beginning Business Workshop—each for a modest fee.

Counselors from SCORE and SBDC

You can make an appointment to speak with someone from the Service Corps of Retired Executives (SCORE), as well as a counselor from your nearest SBDC. Both organizations, sponsored by the Small Business Administration (SBA), offer professional advice for entrepreneurs just starting out in business.

Why spend your time talking to two different counselors? Because they may have totally different areas of advice to give you, and all of it is worth your while. The people at

SCORE, for example, are retired executives who've spent many years managing successful businesses. Some of these men and women will have owned their own businesses, while others will have been high-level employees of major corporations. On the other hand, the counselors at the Small Business Development Centers will have been involved in smaller businesses, perhaps not too different from the one you're planning to operate.

Although it's highly unlikely that you'll be assigned to anyone who has ever managed a home-based antiques business, the consultants who work with you will have had hands-on experience in *some* business. They can give you excellent information on how to set up and operate your shop. They'll walk you through many of the topics you'll read about in this book. They'll play devil's advocate to help you think through any problems you perhaps haven't considered in your enthusiasm to open your shop, and they'll give you an understanding of some basic management procedures, including writing the business plan that's described in Chapter 3.

You'll almost certainly be advised to estimate the amount of cash you'll need to take care of your personal living expenses for at least six months—you may begin making a profit before that, but don't count on it. They'll tell you to look back at what you spent last year for rent or mortgage payments, utilities, food, car payments, clothing, medical expenses, entertainment, taxes, and so forth. Then, in addition to what you'll need for start-up expenses, plan to have that much cash in the bank—or readily available—so that you can draw on it immediately.

These counselors can also give you some government publications to study at home. You'll leave the meetings with a much better understanding of the nitty-gritty part of business, the part that can make or break you as a dealer.

To make an appointment with a SCORE representative or someone from the SBDC, call the SBA office number listed in the U.S. Government section of your telephone directory. In case there's no SBA office near you, call (800) 827–5722 (the SBA Hotline Desk) and ask to have the *Small Business Resource Guide* for your state sent to you. This free guide lists dozens of helpful publications you can order for nominal fees. You can also check with a nearby college. Many have affiliations with an SBDC.

Check Your Local Library

Your counselors might suggest you then pay a visit to your local library for some in-depth research about antiques shops in particular. The reference librarian there will be happy to give you a hand in locating some up-to-date information sources.

One place to start is the *Reader's Guide to Business Periodicals.* This directory catalogs hundreds of current articles about every business subject under the sun. You might very well find listed a few well-written articles that give statistics about the status of the antiques business. Some of these articles might discuss trends, turnover rates, problems the industry is having, and other highly relevant topics.

In almost every case these articles will include quotations from experts in the field of antiques. Jot down the names of the authors of the articles and the experts quoted. You can nearly always get these people's address or telephone numbers by writing to the magazines. Contact these men and women and ask if they could help you with more information. You'll be surprised how accommodating they can be. But be aware that they're also busy people, so be as efficient as possible and send a list of questions by regular mail or e-mail.

Some of the questions you might ask: *What's a reasonable turnover rate for a shop of XX square feet? What are the best advertising media for a home-based antiques shop? How do I build a strong and loyal customer base? If I start with and maintain an inventory of $XXXXX, what can I reasonably expect in revenue?* Make the questions specific to *your* shop. I guarantee that if these experts don't know the answers, they'll refer you to someone who does. I never cease to be amazed at how helpful knowledgeable people can be.

Licenses and Permits

Virtually every town in this country requires the owner of a business to apply for and receive a business license or permit before actually opening her doors. This permit is formal permission to operate your antiques business in your home.

The process for getting this permit isn't involved, but having one is absolutely necessary to carry on a business legally. In most cases all you'll have to do to start the process is fill out a form that asks for the type of business you plan to operate, your name, and the business address.

In your case the only hurdle you might have to jump after that is the fact that you'll be running a business out of your *home*, not from a commercial location. Some communities have strict laws about what businesses can and can't be operated in a residential neighborhood. You might run up against a zoning law that prohibits or restricts home-based retail shops. Whether or not you're in the clear depends to a large extent on your town's attitude toward home-based businesses and the zoning of your neighborhood. Some neighborhoods are zoned for single-family homes only; others allow multiple residential units. And still others allow many types of small businesses right along with residential homes.

So before you go any further, visit your city hall or local township building and explain your plans to someone in the business licenses or planning department. That person can walk you through the zoning regulations that spell out activities permitted in your neighborhood.

Some regulations that apply to you as a home-based dealer in antiques may include the size and placement of signs on the building itself or near the street, the number of parking places available to customers, how much alteration of the home itself will be necessary to accommodate the business, the approximate number of customers who will visit the shop per day, the number of employees you can hire, and so forth. In some towns the planning department schedules a meeting with or a survey of neighbors to approve a home-based business. Almost certainly, there'll be an on-site inspection of your home by a fire marshal.

Suppose you're turned down for your business permit. This isn't likely to happen unless you live in a neighborhood zoned for single-family homes *and* in an exceptionally restrictive town. But if it does, are you out of luck? Not necessarily. Ask any builder or contractor. They routinely appeal turndowns, and the rate of reversal on applications is often good.

If you're not well versed in the vagaries of municipal regulations, your first step in getting that refusal reversed would be to find a local attorney who specializes in obtaining licenses and permits. She will probably tell you that you have two options: (1) You can apply to the appeals board for a review of your application, or (2) you can ask for a variance or exception to whatever rule tripped you up.

Be prepared to state your case politely, clearly, and firmly before a group of people from some city department. Emphasize that your antiques shop will be a nonpolluting, low-traffic impact, quiet business that will be a genuine asset to the community. Show your plans for landscaping and any remodeling of the building. Explain that your shop will be open only during regular business hours. Tell them you plan to be an active, contributing member of the local business community by joining the chamber of commerce, a service club, or other professional organizations. All this will show you to be a responsible person who will operate an attractive, desirable business.

With the growing trend toward home-based businesses of all kinds, your chances of winning are good. Once you're approved for the permit, you'll be required to register your business name.

If you strike out completely on zoning, read Chapter 6, page 137, for an alternative.

Your Business Name

Probably the first thing you decided on, way back when you got the idea for a home-based antiques shop, was the name of your shop. Right? After all, that's the most personal part of this whole business. The name you choose reflects you and how you plan to operate your shop. It shows whether you'll be a cozy little "Grandma's Attic" type of shop or one that blends into the general commercial fabric of the town. Whatever type of shop you choose, be flexible about the name and be willing to change your mind about your first choice. A company's name is a very important part of its image, and once you make the decision, the name will be with you for a long time.

One good idea is to make a list of all the names you might even conceivably call your shop. Brainstorm with your family and friends to come up with fifteen or twenty names. Go over the list and immediately eliminate any that don't appeal to you. Put the list away for a day or so and go back to it. You'll probably be able to eliminate most of the remaining names. Make your choice from the few that are left. Play around with them until you come up with a business name that's really suitable for your shop.

You'll save yourself a little paperwork if you use your own full name, for example, "Laura Colter Antiques," or your initials and your last name, "R. E. Thompson Antiques."

You can, of course, choose what's termed an "assumed business name," such as "Colter and Sons Antiques," "Main Street Antiques," or "Antiques Unlimited," the regulations for which are on the following page. If you decide on an assumed name, and there's absolutely no reason not to, be sure it's one that is descriptive of your shop.

Here are some guidelines for choosing your company name.

1. Your business name should immediately identify your company as one that sells *antiques*. A name such as "Sally's Place" could belong to a fabric shop, a restaurant, a bed-and-breakfast inn, even a copy center! There's no mistaking the business of "Sally's Antiques," however.

2. Does your town already have several antiques shops? Then choose a name that begins with the letter A. Many people look first in the Yellow Pages when searching for a particular service or product. As they run down the list of companies under the category "Antiques Shops," they will naturally see names beginning with A first. So, "Antiques Alley" or "Attic Antiques" would most likely be first on that list.

3. You may want to use your own name as your company name. That's fine as long as your name is easy to spell and pronounce. Granted, the United States is a melting pot, and any telephone book lists plenty of names that, for most people, are difficult to spell and pronounce. If you happen to be the proud possessor of such a name, please consider using an assumed business name, instead.

4. The name should also be one that will differentiate it from other shops in town. Our minds tend to remember the primary word or words in a name and gloss over the less important words. If owners of two shops choose similar names for their shops, customers are going to remember the primary word or words and forget the rest.

    It's easy to see how customers who read an ad placed by a shop called "Country Cousin Antiques" might end up driving to another shop named "Everything Country Antiques," especially if they weren't familiar with either one of them. The primary words *country* and *antiques* in each could be very confusing to them.

5. Your company name should be an accurate indication of the type of merchandise you carry. Will you specialize in high-ticket antiques? Or will you carry moderately priced antiques and collectibles? A name such as "Heirloom Gallery Antiques" might be suitable for the first type of shop, whereas "Aunt Tilly's Attic Antiques" would fit the second one.

If you decide to choose a name other than your own, you'll have to register it with the state as an *assumed business name.* The regulations about business names in most states are pretty standard across the country. They define the terms *assumed business name* and *real and true name* as follows:

- An assumed business name is a name other than the real and true name of each person operating a business. A real and true name becomes an assumed business name with the addition of any words that imply the existence of additional owners. Examples include "Company," "Associates," "Sons" and "Daughters."
- A real and true name is the surname of an individual with the individual's given names(s) or initial(s), or a corporate name or limited partnership name already filed with the state's business registry.

You do not have to register a business name that is a "real and true" name. What's the purpose of registering an assumed business name? It's just to let the public know who is transacting business under that business name.

An assumed business name must be registered in every county in which a business is located, but this probably won't affect you as a home-based retailer. Failure to register an assumed name can be punished by a fine, so don't overlook this requirement. The fee for registering an assumed business name is moderate, about $10 in most states.

To register your business name (if you use an assumed one), write to the secretary of state's office in your state capital and ask for the proper forms. A clerk in your local city hall or courthouse can give you the address. That person can also walk you through the process of registering the name.

Your Sales Tax Number

Since you'll be managing a retail business, you'll have to get a sales tax number (if you live in a state that charges sales tax on retail purchases). This number allows you to buy antiques for resale without paying a sales tax, and it requires you to collect tax on your own sales. Apply for this number at your local city hall or courthouse.

What About a Logo?

A logo is simply a graphic that you have printed on your business cards, your sign, and any other place where you want to give your business a special identity. Antiques shops use logos that look like rocking chairs, cut-glass goblets, and framed pictures. All are attractive and certainly do add interest to the company names.

You can hire an artist to design and draw a logo for you. A less expensive alternative is to use "clip art." Clip art is line drawings reproduced on CD-ROM or available online. While some designs aren't copyrighted, other are; so it's best to find out before you use the design. If you decide to use clip art, just be sure it's of excellent quality, will reproduce well in print advertising, and will portray the image you wish for your shop.

The chances are good that a print shop won't charge for reproducing clip art on your business cards and stationery. You can, of course, do it yourself using the proper computer software. A sign painter may charge a small fee for including a logo on your signs.

Your Business Structure

Another decision you must make early on in the process of getting started is to determine just what legal structure your business will take. A home-based business can be structured in several ways, depending on these factors:

- the size of the operation
- the number of people involved in the venture

- the need for capital to start the business
- tax advantages or disadvantages

Your accountant will help you decide which is best for your particular situation and prepare any documents that may be necessary. Here is a brief summary of four basic types of structures and their differences.

Sole Proprietorship

Sole proprietorship is the simplest and most economical form of ownership. You can open the business with the least amount of paperwork and bureaucratic hassle, and your attorney and accounting fees (both up-front and ongoing) will usually be less than for other forms of business. You are the sole owner of the business. You make all the decisions, take all the risks, pay all the bills, and enjoy all the profits. Your record keeping for the IRS is minimal. There are income tax advantages for owners of small companies.

The biggest disadvantage to a sole proprietorship is that you're *personally* liable for all debts of the company. Also, the growth of the business is pretty well limited to your own energy, ambition, and finances.

Many owners of small businesses also have problems keeping their personal lives separate from their business affairs, and serious illness can mean the end of the business and the loss of all investment.

Partnership

A partnership is when two or more people own a business jointly. They usually share equally all responsibilities in running the shop and share equally in the profits, assuming each has an equal financial investment in the company. Record keeping is fairly simple, with profits taxed as personal income.

While the sole owner of a shop must make all decisions alone, a partnership has the advantage of two or more heads working together to solve problems. If additional capital is needed for the business, it's sometimes easier to obtain it from two or more partners than one person.

One unique partnership advantage for owners of home-based antiques shops is that it allows one partner to manage the shop while another scouts for antiques at estate sales or auctions or works a booth at an antiques show. Having one partner available to keep the shop open also allows the other partner the freedom to take care of personal or family affairs. This is especially valuable for those people with small children.

As with any relationship, disadvantages do exist in a business partnership. The partners must share the profits, which may be pretty slim for the first few months. If one partner eventually moves away or simply decides she doesn't like running the shop, one must buy the other out. This can mean a substantial outlay of cash.

There's always the possibility of a personality conflict, too. Two people who've been lifelong friends, or even close relatives, can discover irritating personality quirks in each other once they're in business together.

Family-Owned Business

A family-owned business may seem to be the ideal partnership. After all, it provides income for two or more family members and keeps the money in the family. In a perfect world that's the way it would work, and it sometime *does* work. Many home-based antiques shops are jointly owned by husband and wife, two sisters, mother and daughter, or some other combination of family members.

Unfortunately, it doesn't always work so well. Emotions can run high in families, and this easily causes sparks when it comes time to make important business decisions. One person may be a strong advocate of the "Advertise, advertise, advertise!" school of business, whereas the other thinks advertising is a waste of good money. Even worse are the situations where family members are brought into the business not because they know anything about selling antiques but simply because they need something to keep them occupied. That's just a disaster waiting to happen! So, think long and hard about sharing your shop with another family member. No one wants to damage family relationships over business.

If, however, you and a relative do plan to operate your shop as partners, you need to establish some definite guidelines long before you open your doors:

- First, agree on the purpose of the shop. Is it to provide the sole income of the partners, or will it serve as an adjunct to other income? The answer to this question might determine the amount spent on remodeling the home, the number of days and hours the shop is open, the promotion and advertising budget, and a dozen other facets of the business.

- Will all partners share in *all* responsibilities of running the shop, or will there be a division of labor and responsibilities? Often one partner will be a great salesperson, for example, while another couldn't sell a Lalique perfume bottle for $5.00 but might have a real talent for locating and *buying* antiques that can be sold at a profit.
- Can you forgo traditional family relationships—mother-daughter or father-son, for example—and work together as *business* partners, not as parent and child? To do so requires a strong sense of independence and a great deal of respect between two people.
- Finally, can you separate your working lives from your personal lives? The problems of home should not encroach on the hours at work, and the problems that arise in the shop should be forgotten, at least temporarily, when you hang out that CLOSED sign at the end of the day.

With loyalty, affection, and effort, a family partnership certainly can work. If this is your plan, enjoy your business and work together for everyone's happiness and financial well-being.

Corporation

Few small-business owners incorporate their companies today, especially in the first years of operation. There was a time when laws gave the owners of corporations broad protections. Those owners couldn't be sued for debts incurred by the corporation or for liabilities that sometimes ran into millions of dollars. Owners of incorporated businesses also received highly favorable advantages when the tax man came around with his hand out. Those days are gone. The few advantages for the small-business person today are outweighed by some of Uncle Sam's stringent rules. Corporations must hold formal meetings, keep endless records, and wade through a morass of red tape. It's hardly ever worth the hassle for an antiques dealer.

Paid Professionals

Your antiques shop may be just a converted garage or living room at first. You may have no employees and plan on a low-key operation for some time. Even so, you'll find it to your advantage to establish working relationships with several professional counselors.

Many people going into business for the first time are reluctant to hire professional counselors. They've had little need in the past for an accountant or an attorney, and their banking and insurance needs have been minimal. They may not know how to choose good professionals or what to expect from their services. They may not see the *need* for these services, which can, admittedly, be expensive. In the long run, however, you'll actually save money by adding these men and women to your operation. They can show you ways to cut your tax bill. They can help you establish a legal business structure that is right for your lifestyle and personal situation. They can set up a simple bookkeeping system for you that you can maintain yourself.

The following section discusses your banker, your insurance agent, your accountant, and your attorney. You might want to interview two or three counselors in each category before settling on one. Be honest with them about exactly what your business encompasses, and expect straight answers from them about fees and what you'll get for your money.

Your Bank and Banker

Plan to open a business checking account separate from your personal one. You'll find it infinitely easier to reconcile expenses and deposits that way.

You may already have a good working relationship with an officer at your current bank. If so, continue with that bank. If for any reason you need to shop for bank services, check out a small, locally owned, full-service bank. Many people have had unsatisfactory experiences when dealing with a branch of a large national bank. By dealing with a smaller bank, where you're known by sight and name, you'll get better, faster, more personal service than from an institution where you're just an account number.

Don't select a bank just because it's the closest one to your home/shop, either. Although that may be convenient as far as making deposits and so forth, you need a bank that has a healthy attitude toward small businesses. Not all of them do. Larger banks, used to dealing with larger businesses, often refuse to make loans of less than $50,000. As an antiques dealer, you may need to borrow $10,000 or less. Find out the bank's attitude about expansion loans for small businesses *before* you open an account.

Your Insurance Agent

You definitely need liability, theft, and fire coverage for your shop, plus coverage on any vehicle you use in the business. You may also want to consider business interruption insurance, health and life insurance, and disability coverage. If you're satisfied with the agent who writes your personal automobile and homeowner's insurance, go to her first. Agents, however, usually work with only one company, and not all companies provide all types of insurance.

If your own agent can't write policies for everything you need, shop around among the insurance brokers in your town. Brokers deal with many companies, not just one, and they'll research the entire industry until they can put together a package that gives you the coverage you need.

Ask each broker to give you a bid that covers the entire package. You'll probably get widely differing figures, so study each package carefully to determine which is the best deal for your particular needs.

Your Accountant

If you've always plowed through the IRS regulations necessary to file your own income tax forms, you may never have felt the need for an accountant. Being in business is a different matter. You can hardly conduct a business efficiently today without the advice and guidance of a qualified accountant.

Don't confuse the services of a bookkeeper with those of an accountant. A bookkeeper simply records expenses and receipts in one or more ledgers. (By using the information in Chapter 4, you can easily handle that responsibility yourself if you care to.) An accountant, on the other hand, prepares your tax returns for you, sets up your schedule of estimated tax payments, and prepares information about deductible expenses and depreciation on capital assets. She can also double-check your bookkeeping system to make sure you're taking advantage of every legal break the government gives small-business people.

One word of advice about selecting an accountant: Choose one who is qualified to handle all the intricate ins and outs of small-business accounting. Basically, you'll find three types of accountants available:

1. *Enrolled Agent* (EA): a person who has passed a two-day exam prepared by the IRS, covering several areas of taxation. This person will probably advertise as a tax specialist.
2. *Accredited Accountant:* a person who has passed an exam prepared by the Accreditation Council of Accountancy and Taxation. These accountants may specialize in small-business accounting.
3. *Certified Public Accountant* (CPA): a person who has passed the American Institute of Certified Public Accountants' rigorous national examination on accounting, auditing, law, and related areas. These professionals must also complete additional training every year to keep up with constantly changing rules regarding taxes and all the other financial matters that affect businesspeople.

Of these three, the best choice for a small business is a CPA. While a CPA's fees may seem high, you'll find the advice will more than pay for itself in tax savings and profits.

A friend in business might be able to recommend an accountant. Accountants are also listed in the Yellow Pages. One of the most important criteria in choosing an accountant, however, is that she have *extensive experience* working with small businesses. This is vital, because the needs of the person managing a small business are quite different from those of individuals or of people who own large corporations. Any accountant you interview should be able to give you references from other clients and should deal with you openly about fees. The accountant should also be willing to come to your shop occasionally if you feel you need on-site help.

Your Attorney

An attorney can advise you about the many small legal aspects of a shop in your home. Most of these details will be simple ones that relate to local regulations, but an attorney can also show you how to protect yourself in case of a lawsuit based on a customer's having an accident on your property. Although the chances of any such litigation are slender, it's always wise to have established a personal relationship with an attorney *in advance.*

If your business is to be managed as a partnership, you should work out the details with an attorney. A simple covenant agreed upon *in advance* can save a lot of misunderstandings later on. This includes partnerships between two or more family members.

Your local bar association may have a referral service that can give you the names of several local attorneys. The number should be in the Yellow Pages, probably the last category under "Attorneys." Not all attorneys, however, are listed with a referral service, so a recommendation from an existing client may be the best way to choose and retain an attorney. Ask your banker, your CPA, or a friend who is in business for recommendations. As with the CPA, the attorney you choose should specialize in working with small businesses.

The fees of both accountants and attorneys vary widely, so don't hesitate to ask what their hourly rate is right up front. Those who are associated with large firms usually charge the highest rates. They must support large staffs and expensive locations and usually deal with people whose needs are quite complicated. As a person in a small business with simple requirements, you'll probably find an accountant or attorney in a one- or two-person office a more affordable choice.

The services of these professionals can be expensive since most charge by the hour. If you have a list of questions or concerns *written out* and ready to discuss at your first meetings with them, you'll probably be able to wrap up all your preliminary needs in an hour.

Build a Customer Base Before You Open

It is hoped that you've sold antiques in some way before opening your own shop. This could have been working in someone else's shop as a salesperson, operating a booth in an antiques mall, owning part of a co-op, or selling at flea markets that specialize in antiques. If so, then you probably already know many of the people in your town who can become *your* customers. Buy a pad with lined pages and start now making a list of these people. Keep the pad handy and add to the list every time you remember a name or contact. By the time you have your grand opening (as described in Chapter 9), you'll have a fine list of ready customers to invite to this very special event.

Estimating Start-up Costs

Chapter 1 recommended that you have enough cash—in the bank or readily available from nonloan sources—to get your business off the ground. You'll need that cash now for the necessary remodeling and other expenses you'll face before you actually open your doors.

Counselors with the Small Business Development Center strongly suggest that you avoid using credit cards for these start-up costs. They advise paying as you go in case you find it difficult to make even minimum payments during your first months in business.

Let's consider some start-up projects.

Walls and Partitions

You may be lucky enough to have a large living room/dining room area where you can display your antiques in style. If so, send up a couple of cheers—you've just lowered your start-up costs by many dollars. If, however, your rooms appear to be a little crowded now with just the family furniture, they're going to be a lot worse when you fill them with antiques. Better plan on taking out a wall or partition to open up some walking-around space.

Instead of turning two rooms into one large room, though, you might consider leaving a foot or two on each side of one original wall intact to form an archway, which is an attractive architectural feature. Even though the two original rooms are now, for all intents and purposes, one room, the archway can serve to divide *types* of antiques. Chapter 8 further describes this.

Carpeting

I suggest you take up any existing residential-type carpeting in your display rooms. You know how hard it is to keep carpeting clean with just the family running in and out. I guarantee it'll be a hundred times worse with *customers* bringing in dirt, mud, and slush on their shoes, and you can't yell, "Clean your feet before you come in!" at customers.

You may have a good wooden floor underneath the carpet. It doesn't have to be hardwood, just firm and solid. If so, all you have to do is sand it smooth and give it a few coats of tough floor varnish. The warm wooden tones will be a perfect complement to your antique furniture.

If you find a composition base under the carpet, you can cover it with a good-quality vinyl flooring. I've seen antiques shops floored with a charming nongloss, deeply textured, brick pattern vinyl that is very effective. Throw a few attractive rugs over this flooring and you have a perfectly acceptable and easy-to-clean background for your antiques. But be sure any area rugs you lay down have an anti-slip backing to prevent customers from slipping or tripping on them, falling, and eventually suing you.

If you really want carpeting, get the hard-finish, low-looped style that's popular with churches, schools, and professional people. This kind will take an incredible amount of punishment and is relatively easy to clean.

Window Coverings

Remove heavy draperies. You need all the light you can get in your shop. Customers always prefer shopping in a place that's light and airy. Replace the draperies with lace curtains, checkered cafe curtains, or anything else that will carry through an ambience of nostalgia.

Electrical Wiring

Your permit may require you to install modern wiring if your house was built many decades ago. Don't resent this expense. It will actually add to the value of your house, should you decide to sell it someday.

Light Fixtures

Whether or not you have to replace old wiring with new, you'll probably need to arrange for additional overhead light. Without it, your shop will be gloomy and depressing on dark winter days. Track or recessed lighting around the perimeter of your rooms is one solution, and so are fluorescent tubes hidden behind a valance, as described in Chapter 8. For real elegance, you could install chandeliers whose crystal prisms glitter and glow in the sunlight.

While you're at it, make sure you have enough outlets on the walls. You'll need these for the lamps you stock. Avoid using electical extension cords and consider using power strips with an on/off switch into which you can plug multiple small lamps.

New Drywall and Trim

You may need new drywall and trim to fill in spaces where old walls were removed—not an expensive or difficult job.

Paint or Paper

Once your rooms are enlarged or remodeled, you can paint or paper them any color you like, of course. The obvious choice might seem to be a neutral, such as white, ivory, or light gray. Many dealers, however, find that brighter walls (sky blue, Pepto-Bismol pink, sunflower yellow) add real pizzazz to their shops. I think the reason the colored walls work is that most antique furniture is medium to dark brown—not especially lively tones. If you place such furniture against neutral walls, you get a pretty blah combination of noncolors, and brightly colored paint or paper costs no more than a neutral. The only caveat here is to have plenty of daylight and artificial light to compensate for the colored walls.

Shelving

You'll discover that you will make many more sales of small antiques—glassware, china, silver, and so forth—than you do of large pieces such as furniture. This means you'll need quite a bit of shelving to display these little beauties. The best choice is to order plate-glass shelves from your local glass company. The up-front cost for glass shelves is more than for wooden shelves, but in the long run you'll come out ahead. You don't have to paint or varnish glass, and it cleans easily with window cleaner and a quick swipe with a paper towel. Another advantage of glass is that light shines through it, so the antiques displayed on lower shelves sparkle just as well as the ones on the top shelf.

I like to install glass shelves in windows in place of curtains too. Sunlight pouring through colored glass displayed on glass shelves gives a rainbowlike glow to a room. Also, casual passersby who see your window can't help but be drawn to its beauty. They may come in just to inspect the pretty colored glass.

Exterior Sign

You may have to construct your exterior sign to conform to municipal regulations. Some towns will allow almost any type of sign, while others won't allow one that extends at right angles more than a certain number of feet from the building itself. A few towns regulate the lighting of signs. Some towns, for example, will allow lighted signs but not neon lighting. Be sure to check out any restrictions before you order your sign.

Do order your sign from a professional sign painter. Don't try to save a few dollars by painting it yourself, unless you're an artist. Few things degrade the appearance of a business more than an amateurish, poorly painted sign. Many sign companies today can design a potential sign on their computers and print the result on paper for you to examine. The designer can make changes right before your eyes on the computer until the design is exactly what you want. It's then painted on wood.

As for the actual design of your sign, choose a pattern and lettering that convey the image of an earlier era. Avoid thin, spidery-looking letters; they're pretty but very hard to read from the street. Drive around town and simply observe other signs that appeal to you. Then go and do likewise.

If you have a choice, the best type of sign is one that extends at right angles from the building or from a post on the lawn and can be read from both directions. You'll also generate interest and direct customers to your shop if you can place additional signs at corners or intersections.

In addition, you'll need a small sign for the front door that announces the days and hours your shop is open. Many home-based dealers, especially if they don't have family obligations, will also work with serious customers during normally closed hours if the customers call first. Should you want to do that, your sign might read as follows:

OPEN TUESDAY–SATURDAY

9:00–5:00

OR BY APPOINTMENT

555–6793

To be honest, this sign may *not* stop people from knocking on your closed door on Sundays, evenings, holidays, and any other time that suits them. One of the hazards of operating a shop in your home is that a few people seem to rationalize that, since you already live at your place of business, you won't mind opening your shop for a few minutes.

You actually may not mind opening your doors if you're not otherwise engaged. One of my friends who manages an in-home shop has a sign such as the one described above, but it's not attached permanently to the shop door. He has a hook on the door and places the sign there when the shop is closed and he doesn't want to be disturbed. But if, for example, on a Sunday afternoon he's not watching the Super Bowl on television, taking a nap, or entertaining friends at a backyard barbecue, he simply removes the sign. He has a brass bell attached to the inside of the door, and it jangles whenever anyone enters. His living quarters are close enough to the shop area that he can hear the bell easily. That way, he doesn't have to personally monitor the shop area during his off-hours, but if anyone comes in, he's there in seconds to welcome them. As he says, "Why not? I'm in business to make money."

Many home-based dealers have such a bell on their door for other reasons. After all, you're going to have to leave the shop area and go into your living quarters occasionally, for lunch and bathroom breaks if for nothing else.

Exterior Painting

While you're driving around looking for examples of attractive signs, also watch for color combinations on homes or businesses that you think would attract attention and draw customers to your shop. The same philosophy applies here that does to painting the interior walls of your shop: Avoid the neutrals and go for strong colors that make a statement.

If you're a little hesitant about combining bold colors, go to your library and check out a book called *Painted Ladies*. In this great book you'll find dozens of pictures of fancifully painted Victorian homes. While you may not want to get as wild as the paint on some of these old beauties, you'll see how effective strong, contrasting colors can be. By painting your shop in similar tones, I guarantee you'll definitely create some preopening interest that's bound to establish you as an innovative antiques dealer.

Landscaping

Any landscaping around and in front of a home-based shop should be low-key. You don't want to detract from the business side of your shop by having too many large residential-type shrubs and flowers in front of the building. Brick walkways bordered by low-growing flowers, a miniature lawn, and a small tree or two are usually enough. You can always move any cherished roses or other ornamentals to the backyard and enjoy them there. The more appealing your entrance, the more it will attract customers. Avoid high hedges and narrow walkways.

Customer Parking

You may live in a neighborhood where some customers can walk to your shop. Most of them, however, will drive, and they'll need a place to park their cars. You undoubtedly have two or three parking places at the curb in front of the shop, but you don't own the street. Anyone can park there—neighbors, visitors, people going to nearby shops, workmen. These people can easily usurp the parking spaces in front of your shop, leaving no place for your customers to park.

Try to find a way to create even two or three parking places on your premises. Can you remove the turf from your front lawn and pour blacktop there? Is the side yard wide enough to block off a couple of places? Do you have alley access that would let customers park in the rear? Try to come up with something. Anything you do will add to the professional image of your shop, in addition to making it far easier for customers to visit you. This is one expense that can certainly be postponed, however, if you're short of funds.

Office Expenses

Basic Supplies

Do you have a warehouse-type office supply company nearby where you can buy office supplies and paper goods? If you do, you can save a great deal of money by patronizing it. For example, a string of one hundred small price tags at the office supply company in one dealer's town costs $1.99, or about 2 cents each. A warehouse-type company in a town 12 miles away charges $15, or 1½ cents each, for a box of 1,000 of the same tags—a savings of 25 percent. Multiply that savings by all the paper goods you have to buy, and you'll see the advantage of shopping at a warehouse, even if you have to drive some distance every two or three months to replenish your supplies.

Your basic supplies will include the following:

- stringed price tags
- stick-on price tags
- bags (large and small)
- tissue paper for wrapping fragile items
- sales-receipt books
- rubber stamp to imprint your shop name on receipts, invoices, and so forth
- a ledger or two for keeping records

While commercially printed sales receipts, stationery, and so forth, look good, you can save money initially by having a rubber stamp made that shows the name of your shop, your address, your telephone number, and perhaps your e-mail address. You can then buy blank receipt pads and a ream of paper at your office supply store and stamp them to create your own receipts and stationery. An alternative method is to use a computer word processing program to create your own stationery, envelopes, and even receipts, for the cost of the paper and a print cartridge.

Business Cards

Business cards are a great and inexpensive way to advertise your shop and services. You'll put them on your checkout counter, in every bag a customer carries out of the shop, and in numerous other places. Copy centers can print business cards in a rainbow of colors and typeface styles. If your home/shop is not on a well-known street, you might have a map highlighting it printed on the reverse side of the card. Another hint: If you plan to offer appraisals, estate sales, or any other nonshop service, place a line or two on the card to that effect.

You can obtain 250 free business cards on the Internet from VistaPrint (www.vistaprint.com). Although you won't have a lot of choices in designs, the cards are attractive, and you can input whatever information you want on them. The company also offers low-cost premium cards with glossy finishes.

Telephone

You may already have a telephone extension in the part of your home that will be your sales area, which is fine, except that it undoubtedly also rings at any other phone in the house. This is no problem if you live alone or if no one else is in the house during your open hours. Since you'll be using the phone for business, however, your telephone company may require you to get a separate business line regardless of your personal family situation. You're certainly going to want to list your business in the Yellow Pages, and this type of listing may also require a separate business line. Look in the front section of your telephone book for the number to call for information about this matter.

Answering Machine

Granted, most people hate to listen to recorded messages, but the fact remains that an answering machine is a necessity today for anyone in business. You can record a message that lists your open hours, one that describes upcoming special promotions, or anything else you choose. You can change it from day to day if you like.

Of course, you'll pick up the phone if you're right there and available, but that won't always be the case. Some dealers record a message that says something like this: "Hello, this is Kitty Stinson at Kitty's Antiques. I'm either with a customer or away from the shop right now. Please leave your name, phone number, and a brief message, and I'll get back to you as soon as I can. Please wait for the tone."

Before recording your message, practice saying it over and over until your voice sounds relaxed and happy. You can even record music at the beginning and end of your message if you like. Just place a radio tuned to an easy-listening station nearby; turn the volume to an average pitch and start the recording mode on the answering machine. After a second or two, lower the volume on the radio and record your message. At the end of your message, raise the volume on the radio again. This recording procedure will make your message sound professional.

Computer

While a computer isn't absolutely necessary to run an antiques shop, you'll find that having one will make record keeping and correspondence easier. In fact, many dealers today buy and sell online, so, for them, a computer is a necessity. In order not to throw your budget completely off, you should consider purchasing a used computer. For the type of work you'll be doing on it—word processing, spreadsheets for records, accounting, online searches, even sign making—you'll find that a computer with a Pentium II or III processor will work fine. Even though a desktop computer costs less, many antiques dealers who do shows choose to use laptops, so they can keep their records up to date while on the road.

Since many larger businesses lease their computers, these, like cars today, come on the market when the company needs to upgrade. And that gives you the opportunity to buy a computer for just a few hundred dollars, including monitor and keyboard. And since so many people are involved with computers today, you should be able to find someone you know to help you set it up and install the software you need—although often the computers come with software installed.

You'll find some good buys at Web sites like Computer-Show.com (www.computer-show.com), a site that sells lease-back Dell desktop and laptop computers. Or you may want to check for the nearest MarketPro Computer Show (www.marketproshows.com). These monthly shows set up at convention centers throughout the United States and offer discount computers and software. If you do go to one of these shows, it's a good idea to bring along someone who knows about computers to help you find the best buys.

Web Site

Once you get your antiques business started, you may want to consider having a Web site—or, at least, participating in an online antiques mall. Creating a Web site from which to sell your antiques is not something you'll be able to do yourself and it won't be cheap. To begin, you may want to create a simple site that acts as your presence or home on the Internet.

This can show photographs of some of your inventory, as well as note your specialty, address, shop hours, and so forth. This type of site you can easily set up on your own using a free site builder program from Yahoo/Geocities (http://geocities.yahoo.com).

But there's more to Web sites than just creating them. You must find a host for your site. If you're on a very limited budget, you may want to opt for a free site from Yahoo/Geocities. However, this comes with a small ad, which a visitor can remove, that Yahoo places on your site. For a site without an ad, you'll have to pay a fee. This also applies to sites at Tripod (www.tripod.lycos.com), which also offers free sites.

To set up a commercial site—one from which you sell your antiques and collectibles— you'll have to not only pay a Web designer about $100 per page to create it, but you'll also have to pay more for hosting your site since you'll need a secure site to prevent identity theft. So you may want to wait until your business takes off a bit to undertake this.

An alternative to having a full commercial site is to become a seller in an online antiques mall like TIAS (www.tias.com). Here, you'll pay a monthly fee for an online "shop," which is networked to other dealers' shops at TIAS. This may work out better in the long run if your business is a small operation.

Business Checks

Most owners of small businesses find the three-checks-to-a-page system quite adequate. Beside each check is a section for recording the amount of the check, to whom it was written, for what it was written, and the date. This system makes record keeping simple and fast.

Credit Card Affiliation

There's no getting around the fact that being a credit card merchant is to your advantage as a retailer. One survey showed that you can actually increase your sales by 11 percent if you accept credit cards.

A few years ago many owners of new businesses encountered a great deal of trouble qualifying to become credit card merchants. Some owners had to wait up to a year before a bank would even consider their applications. Banks felt it took that long to establish an acceptable credit rating. In most cases that scenario doesn't exist today. Almost any person with a good personal credit record can apply to become a credit card merchant now.

Merchant Information Sheet

Please supply the following merchant information:

Date: _____

  1. Business Structure: (circle one)

      Sole Proprietorship   Partnership   Corporation   Nonprofit

  2. Merchant Name (DBA) _____

  3. Contact Person _____

  4. Business Phone _____ Business Fax _____

  5. Physical Address _____

  6. Mailing Address _____

  7. E-mail Address _____

  8. Federal Tax ID or SS# (if sole proprietorship) _____

  9. Owner's Information/100% ownership

    Name _____

    Address _____

    % of ownership _____ Home Phone _____ SS# _____

    Name _____

    Address _____

    % of ownership _____ Home Phone _____ SS# _____

    Name _____

    Address _____

    % of ownership _____ Home Phone _____ SS# _____

10. Current Processor
    Please fax 2-3 months current business checking account statements if new business.

11. Referral Bank _____ Branch _____

    Contact _____

It will cost you something to use an electronic terminal for credit card purchases in your shop. You'll just have to decide if your budget can handle that expense at first. It's best to find a place for the terminal in your budget as soon as possible. Doing so will definitely increase your sales.

To apply for an electronic terminal, you must go to your local banker. She will ask you to fill out a form, such as the one on the previous page. You'll be told that you have several options available—renting, leasing, or buying a terminal. Some expensive terminals handle large volumes of business. Other less expensive ones are ideal for merchants whose credit card purchases are smaller. Unless you're dealing in high-end antiques, you'll probably want the latter type.

Once your bank approves your credit, your application will be sent to the processing center. A technician will then come to your shop to install the terminal.

Every time you run a customer's card through your terminal, the processing center will record the dollar amount of the purchase in the customer's credit card account. That amount will be automatically deposited into your own business account.

General Business Expenses

Trade Journal Subscriptions

As a dealer, you must stay ahead of your customers where trends are concerned, and trade journals are a source of helpful information. A dozen times a week you'll have to refer to price guides for help in pricing an item. You also need to get hints on shop management from the experiences of other dealers. You'll find all this information in books and publications read by dealers in antiques. (Many of these publications are listed in the Appendix.)

Business Memberships

Chamber of Commerce. You'll probably find it to your advantage to belong to your local chamber of commerce. This organization holds meetings where knowledgeable consultants and professionals in many fields speak on business-related topics. The chamber of commerce also sponsors social events where you're encouraged to network and promote your business to other members. As a member, you'll receive a window sticker that identifies you to customers as a responsible member of the business community. Although membership fees differ from town to town and region to region around the country, the average is about $125 per year.

Service Clubs. You might also want to consider membership in a service club such as Rotary, Kiwanis, or Lions. These are clubs for businesspeople with the purpose of increasing skills, knowledge, and visibility in the community. Membership fees for these clubs vary greatly from town to town.

If you're at all hesitant about joining a business organization, just ask if you can attend a meeting or two as a guest. You'll learn very quickly what the responsibilities and advantages of membership may be.

Business License

In most communities the fees for the various permits and licenses you'll need to open your shop run between $25 and $75 each. Call the permit and license department at your city hall to find out the exact figures for your town.

Attorney and CPA Fees

I suggest that you spend at least an hour with an attorney and a CPA as part of your pre-opening process. These professionals price their time by the hour, and the rates vary widely from region to region. It pays to call several of each to get an idea of local rates.

Insurance

You also need good insurance coverage. I can only suggest that you call the agent who handles your existing homeowner's insurance or an insurance broker and find out what additional coverage for your shop will cost.

Advertising

You should do some advertising for your grand opening. Budget for a large display ad in your local newspaper for this important event. This ad is vital to letting potential customers know you're in business. The clerk at the newspaper's advertising desk can tell you exactly what such an ad would cost.

Truck or Van

With any kind of luck, you already own some type of vehicle that you can use to haul antique furniture to your shop. You may decide to deliver some pieces for your customers, which will also require a truck or van. In any event, you have to have one. One word of advice: If you have to buy a vehicle, don't go out and buy an expensive new one. The payments will cut too deeply into your profits. Don't make the mistake of overspending in the beginning. Find a good used truck or van at a lot or from an ad in the paper. Have it inspected at a diagnostic center before you invest your cash. You'll be ahead of the game. No one is going to judge the quality of your shop by the amount of shiny chrome on your delivery truck.

Projecting Your Start-up Costs

To help you project your start-up costs, use the chart on page 47, which lists most of your projected expenses. Do a little research and estimate what each will cost you. Depending upon the layout of your home and the requirements of obtaining your permit, you may have to do less or more actual remodeling. Try your best to hold down expenses by doing as much of the remodeling work as you physically and legally can.

Best Time to Open Your Shop

If you have a choice about the best season to open your shop, I'd suggest spring. Statistically, most dealers do the largest portion of their business between Memorial Day and the winter holidays, unless you live in Arizona or another area where summer is the low season. By opening early in the year, you have a chance to develop a strong customer base before the heavy buying season starts.

Four Steps to a Successful Beginning

Before you charge ahead with your plans, study carefully these four steps to a successful beginning:

1. *Write down your goals.* Sit down and write a few sentences that will describe exactly what you plan to accomplish with your antiques shop. Will it provide you with an income to supplement an existing source of funds? Or will the shop, in time, be your sole source of income? If so, when? Will the selling space remain the same, or do you plan to expand as your customer base and income increase? If so, when and how much? How much money do you plan (not hope) to make within a specified length of time? When and how much?

   Make your statements positive. "I will by September of 20___ own an antiques shop that is grossing $_____ per year in revenue. I will accomplish this goal by maintaining an inventory of no less than $_____ of quality antiques and collectibles and by spending a minimum of ten hours every week pursuing an aggressive marketing plan."

   Type these statements and tape them on your dresser or bathroom mirror, where you'll see them every day. They'll then become transformed from a dream into an attainable goal. You won't be sidetracked when you have this statement to guide you every day.

2. *Put fear aside.* Don't become a victim of the What If syndrome: What if there's a depression and I lose all my money? What if I don't really know how to manage a shop? What if I can't keep the shop stocked? What if my family feels I'm neglecting it? What if . . . ? What if . . . ? What if . . . ?

   You'll accomplish nothing great if you allow fear and doubt to stand in the way of your dreams. George Washington would never have made it across the

Start-up Costs

(Ignore any that don't apply to you and add any you feel will be necessary for your business.)

Removing any walls or partitions to enlarge selling area $ _____

Removing carpeting and/or draperies $ _____

Refinishing or recovering floors $ _____

Upgrading existing electrical wiring to satisfy codes $ _____

New light fixtures $ _____

New drywall and trim $ _____

Repainting interior walls and trim $ _____

New window coverings $ _____

Shelving $ _____

Exterior sign $ _____

Exterior painting $ _____

Landscaping $ _____

Parking area $ _____

Office supplies $ _____

Computer $ _____

Business cards $ _____

Business telephone line $ _____

Answering machine $ _____

Business checks $ _____

Credit card membership (if any) $ _____

Subscriptions to trade journals $ _____

Business memberships $ _____

Business license $ _____

Initial attorney and CPA fees $ _____

Insurance $ _____

Initial advertising $ _____

Truck or van $ _____

Total Projected Start-up Costs $ _____

Add the total of your projected start-up costs to the amount you think you'll need to live for six months and you have the total you should have in the bank or readily available for immediate use.

Delaware River if he'd worried, "What if the boat leaks and we all drown?" Stanley would never have found Livingstone if he'd feared, "What if I get eaten by a lion?" Babe Ruth would never have hit 714 home runs if he'd panicked, "What if I strike out?" every time a ball came his way. Katharine Hepburn would never have won four Academy Awards if she'd quivered, "What if I forget my lines?" Great things can be accomplished by ordinary people just like you and me if we only have faith in ourselves.

3. *Plan ahead.* Take positive steps toward owning your own shop. Attend antiques shows and talk with the exhibitors. Ask them what's selling at what prices. Go to auctions and watch the dealers bid. What are they buying and at what prices? Cruise the antiques shops in your area regularly and observe their display and merchandising methods. Watch the papers and see how other shops advertise.

   Spend every dollar you can spare on inventory for your shop. Fill your closets, your garage, your attic, and your guest bedroom with boxes and accessories and furniture ready to sell.

   Build up a substantial savings account to use for start-up expenses, or prepare to transfer funds from investment sources to a savings account.

4. *Finally, and most important, act as though you already own a successful antiques shop!* Say to yourself, and to anyone who asks, "I own an antiques shop." In your own mind see yourself hanging out the OPEN sign every morning. Visualize customers flocking to your shop. See them picking up antiques and bringing them to your checkout counter. Imagine your cash box full of money.

   Believe you're *already* successful, and you will be successful!

Chapter Three

Your Business Plan

You look at the title of this chapter, shake your head, and wonder, "My business plan?" You may never have written a business plan in your life. Let's face it—before you opened this book, you may never have heard of a business plan. You're probably thinking: (1) What is this thing? (2) What's it for? (3) Why do I need one? and (4) How do I put one together? Well, here are your answers.

What Is a Business Plan?

A business plan is a detailed description of who you are and what your basis is for operating your antiques shop, how you plan to manage it, how you will finance it, what its projections for success are, which professionals will assist you, and what overall direction you plan to take in the years to come.

Why Is a Business Plan Necessary?

Constructing a business plan may seem like an awful lot of work because you have to do hours of research before you begin writing, but there are several good reasons for you to write a business plan.

1. *First and most important, constructing a business plan will force you to look at every aspect of operating a home-based antiques shop.* Before you complete the

plan outline in this book, or any other business plan outline, you must work your way through dozens of details—some minor, some major—that are essential to the successful operation of an antiques shop. Every one of these elements is covered in some chapter of this book, so even though the plan is described here in Chapter 3, you need to study the entire book before starting to construct your plan.

You know antiques—that's a given. You probably know how to sell them too. But to be successful as the owner of a shop, you also have to understand such things as demographics, bookkeeping, promotion, and a dozen other aspects of any successful business. As you complete, one by one, all the necessary steps, from getting that first permit to planning your grand opening, you'll be gathering the information you need to write your business plan.

2. *A business plan will help you determine whether enough people in your town might actually become your customers.* Perhaps you've never owned an antiques shop before but doing so has been a dream for many years. Great! Your enthusiasm for opening a home-based shop, however, isn't enough to guarantee success. There must be a need for the shop in your area.

3. *A business plan becomes a guide to help you manage your shop efficiently.* You'll make your day-to-day decisions proactively based on a previously organized plan rather than reactively based on unrelated events or spur-of-the-moment choices.

This plan won't be just a boring document that you write, then stick in a drawer somewhere in the storeroom. It will become a blueprint you'll use to guide your decision-making processes in years to come. Nothing in it will be written in concrete. As time passes and you see problems with your initial concepts, or opportunities you missed at first, you can go back and adapt the plan to current needs. The plan will provide you with the tools for analyzing your business and for any changes that become necessary. Most counselors recommend that you reevaluate your business and adapt your plan to accommodate changes every year.

The graphic below shows how such a system works:

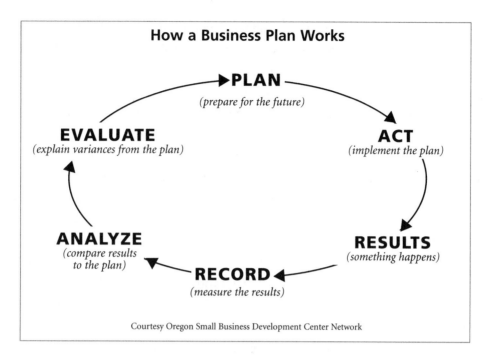

How a Business Plan Works

➤**PLAN**
(prepare for the future)

EVALUATE
(explain variances from the plan)

ACT
(implement the plan)

ANALYZE
(compare results to the plan)

RESULTS
(something happens)

RECORD
(measure the results)

Courtesy Oregon Small Business Development Center Network

As you can see, by following the arrows, you decide on a course of action—opening your shop—then put the plan into effect. Events begin to happen—customers come to the shop and buy your antiques. You record the results of those events—you make a profit or you don't. You study the figures on your monthly balance sheets to determine whether your original projections are working. If they aren't, you determine the reason (prices too low, markup ratio not high enough, incorrect inventory, too little advertising, and so forth). You adjust your original plan to accommodate the results of this evaluation. You then have a new, revised plan to work with for the current year. Your revised plan will help you take advantage of practices that resulted in a profit and will eliminate or modify those that didn't.

Obviously, a great deal of thought must go into this evaluation, which is in reality *a plan for success.* Nobody plans to fail, but you will fail if you fail to plan. That old saying may be corny but, unfortunately, it's true. Many business failures are due not to lack of a good product or expertise on the part of the owner but to poor management. This plan will help you be a better manager of your shop. In other words, researching all the data needed for this plan will force you to think through many critical aspects of your business that you might otherwise overlook. It will help you anticipate the future, make well-informed decisions, and then act on those decisions.

4. *Your business plan will be a concrete statement of your financial situation, your short- and long-range goals, and your prospects for success.* You may need such a statement as part of your application for a zoning variance to add parking spaces to your property or to use certain types of outdoor signs. Many municipalities have strict regulations about such things, but can often be persuaded to bend the rules if you can show you're a responsible businessperson and your plans won't detract from the ambience of the neighborhood.

You may someday need to apply for a bank loan to finance an expansion to your selling area or to buy a truck to haul your antiques. Most bankers won't be familiar with the antiques business, and they may be quite leery of lending money for an enterprise they consider marginal. To get any kind of loan, you're going to have to convince them you're in control of your business's future. A well-thought-out business plan can go a long way toward doing just that.

Your business plan will include a *cash flow statement.* Most of us have always maintained some sort of personal budget. We know what our normal monthly expenses will be and what our normal monthly income will be. Without such a budget, we'd surely have too much month left when the money runs out! You'll keep a budget, too, for your business, so you'll have the money to pay your bills and buy stock based on past and projected income. This budget is labeled your "cash flow statement."

Your cash flow statement will have a section for each month of the year. In each monthly section you'll include your *monthly* expenses in running the shop—utilities, advertising, mortgage or rent, automobile expenses. You'll also factor in, for the appropriate months, expenses you have on a quarterly or an annual basis—insurance, taxes, and so forth.

The cash flow statement you include with your business plan will *project* your income for each month. These projections will be based on your research into what other, similar antiques shops are making. Granted, this may not be easy, but your counselors at SCORE and the Small Business Development Center can help you come up with approximate figures.

Once you actually have the shop in operation, you'll adjust these figures to reflect your actual income. The cash flow statement then becomes a tool to predict how much available cash you'll have at any given month. If you know, for example, that your insurance comes due in March and that February is usually a slow month where income is concerned, you'll be careful about buying too much stock in January and February. Otherwise, you may not have the cash to pay for the insurance. The chart on pages 54 and 55 is a typical cash flow statement form for a home-based antiques shop. A copy of this form is in the appendix.

5. Your business plan can alert you to opportunities for profit that you didn't know existed. Chapter 9 has some great ideas for promoting your business, and Chapter 10 details some unique ways you can generate additional income from your knowledge of antiques. You might want to include some of these ideas in your business plan. They'll be there, then, as part of your overall merchandising program.

The time you spend putting a business plan together will pay off tenfold!

How Do You Construct a Business Plan?

To easily learn more about business plan basics, visit the SBA Web site at the following link: www.sba.gov/starting_business/planning/basic.html.

Business Plan Outline for a Home-Based Antiques Business

The outline that follows has been adapted from several suggested business plans. This one is suitable for a small- to medium-size home-based antiques business. It will be easier to relate this outline to your own plan if you can see a completed business plan. With this in mind, beginning on page 60 you'll find a hypothetical plan based on this outline.

Cash Flow Projections

	Jan.	Feb.	Mar.	Apr.	May	
1. Beginning Cash Balance						
2. Cash Receipts						
a. Cash sales						
b. Estate sales						
c. Appraisals						
d. Consignments						
e. Other						
3. Total Cash Receipts						
4. Cash Disbursements						
a. Merchandise						
b. Accounting						
c. Advertising						
d. Auto expense						
e. Contributions						
f. Delivery expenses						
g. Electricity						
h. Heat						
i. Insurance						
j. Laundry						
k. Legal expenses						
l. Miscellaneous expenses						
m. Office expenses						
n. Postage						
o. Rent/mortgage						
p. Repairs						
q. Telephone						
r. Dues/subscriptions						
s. Travel expenses						
t. Estimated tax payments						
u. Owner withdrawal						
5. Net Cash Flow						
6. Ending Cash Balance						

	June	July	Aug.	Sept.	Oct.	Nov.	Dec.

Cover Page: Include your business name, address, and telephone number; the date the plan is completed; and your name as owner. Type this information, centered, on one sheet.

Table of Contents: This page shows the major topics of your plan and the page numbers they are on.

Mission Statement: This is a brief, positive statement of your philosophy about dealing in antiques. It should express the main reason you chose to open a home-based antiques shop rather than some other type of business—a child-care center, florist shop, bakery, watch-repair shop, and so forth.

Description of Antiques Business: This covers details about the antiques business in general.

Description of Your Antiques Shop: This section describes the types of antiques you plan to sell. Will you carry a variety of antiques from all periods, or will you specialize in one or two eras? Will you carry some reproductions? Will you carry nonantiques, such as reference books or polishes?

Do you plan to appraise antiques (on an informal basis) for your customers? Will you manage estate sales for local people? Will you take in consignments?

Management: This section includes personal data about you as the owner of your shop. Include your background in antiques, your retailing experience, and any education you have in marketing. Include your

1. skills
2. experience

Timing of Opening the Shop: Why did you choose a certain month or season to open your shop?

Location of Your Home/Shop: You may open your shop in the home you've lived in for years or buy a house with the specific purpose of creating a home-based antiques shop there. In either case this section contains information about the neighborhood, the traffic count of the street, and the advantages and disadvantages of that particular location. You'll also include information about the demographics of your shopping area and the size and potential of the market.

Market for Your Products and Services: Here you describe the results of your demographic studies. What is the current population in your town? the median income level? the interest in antiques among those with discretionary income?

Competition: If your area is a viable market for antiques, then other antiques shops probably already exist there. How many others are there? Where are they located? Do they appear to be successful? How will your shop differ from them? What are the special features about your shop that will make it fill a niche in the antiques market? Include

1. strengths and weaknesses
2. comparisons with competition

Projected Financial Success: No one can predict exactly how a business will do in its first year or two, but an educated guess can be made based on the business climate of a town and the success of similar firms.

Analysis of Potential Problems: Here you'll describe any problems you foresee in managing your shop and the way you plan to overcome them.

Short- and Long-Term Goals: It's axiomatic that businesspeople who set reasonable goals for their businesses and let nothing deter them from the path to those goals will succeed. It's just as important, too, to *put those goals on paper!* Somehow, writing goals down almost guarantees they'll be achieved.

Your plan will contain short-term goals for your first year in business and longer-term goals of two to five years. Since a business plan is an ongoing guide, you'll revise your goals every year.

Avoid writing abstract goals, such as "I plan to make great progress in my first year in business." Your goals should be concrete ones that can be measured. Include such things as these:

1. developing a mailing list
2. holding regular promotional events
3. increasing sales volume
4. increasing profit margin
5. expansion plans

Business Structure: Will your business be a sole proprietorship, or will you have a partner?

Professional Counselors: You'll list here the professionals who will assist you in managing your shop efficiently. They will be the following:

1. attorney
2. accountant
3. insurance agent
4. banker

Your Advertising/Promotion Strategy: Your advertising and promotion plans, like the overall business plan, are guides you'll follow on a month-to-month basis. They contain the following:

1. your targeted advertising (to specific customers)
2. your general advertising (newspaper ads and the like)
3. where and when you'll buy media space and time
4. your promotion plans for your opening and for the first year
5. your budget for advertising and promotion

Pricing and Service Strategies: Your shop will quickly develop its reputation based primarily on two factors: (1) the quality of your antiques and (2) the prices you charge for those antiques. You may have low or high prices, low- or high-quality merchandise. You'll make these decisions based upon your own market research.

Secondary in importance are the services you offer your customers. Most people shop for price and quality first, but every good businessperson knows that good service can make a positive contribution to your success. Will you offer any special services, such as free delivery or gift wrapping? What about gift certificates?

Financial Data: This is the most critical section of your business plan, and it may seem to be the most formidable to construct.

This section should have all relevant financial data about your business. The figures you use should be as accurate and verifiable as possible. Include the following:

1. sources of funds
    a. savings
    b. loans (if any)
2. use of funds
    a. start-up costs
    b. inventory

3. cash flow projections
4. personal income statement
   a. mortgage or rent payments
   b. equity in home
   c. vehicles owned
   d. personal debt
   e. other income

Sample Business Plan

On the following pages you'll find a business plan for a hypothetical home-based antiques shop. Adapt the information on these pages to reflect the facts about your own business.

Sally's Antiques

123 Oak Drive
YourTown, USA 46822
(805) 555–6938

January 17, 2005

Owner: Sally Johnson

Table of Contents

Mission Statement

Antiques are considered one of the best investments today, and quality antiques nearly always increase in value with time. In addition, antiques bring beauty and pleasure daily to those who use them in their homes. For these reasons I've chosen a career as a dealer in antiques.

Description of Antiques Business

Men and women have collected antiques for centuries, and the antiques business is a stable industry with an overall pattern of growth.

Nostalgia is definitely "in" today, and this trend is a major contributor to the success of antiques dealers. A dozen or more national magazines focus on the charm of yesterday, complete with lavish photographs of homes decorated with antiques. Americans throughout the country and at all income levels are acquiring antiques for their own homes. The vast majority of these antiques are purchased in small- to medium-size shops.

Since antiques are one of a kind, they are not available to dealers from commercial vendors as are average retail items. Astute dealers, therefore, are aware of nontraditional sources for their merchandise. Antiques can be purchased at many of these sources for a fraction of their retail values. This means that markup in antiques shops is usually far higher, and, therefore, more profitable to the dealer, than is possible in the average retail shop.

Description of Sally's Antiques

Sally's Antiques is a new, home-based antiques shop located in the Silver Road district of YourTown. The shop will be located in Ms. Sally Johnson's home, occupying the former living, dining, and breakfast rooms of the home. Ms. Johnson is remodeling these rooms, comprising 600 square feet of space, to adapt them to a shop atmosphere.

In Sally's Antiques Ms. Johnson will carry a wide variety of antiques and collectibles, including but not limited to: primitive furniture, pine and oak furniture, nineteenth-century glassware and china, old baskets, old rugs, miscellaneous jewelry, and paper goods.

In addition to managing her shop, Ms. Johnson will also hold professionally managed public sales for individuals who wish to sell an entire estate of antiques.

Management of Sally's Antiques

Ms. Johnson has been a homemaker for most of her adult life. The family moved frequently because of the requirements of her husband's business. In each new town Ms. Johnson established a comfortable home for the family, using antiques that she bought at local sales and shops. Visitors to her homes always commented on her excellent taste in decorating.

Through the years Ms. Johnson acquired a great deal of knowledge about antiques. As Mr. Johnson neared retirement, Ms. Johnson began an intensive study of antiques in libraries, museums, and antiques shops and at antiques shows. The purpose was to prepare herself to open an antiques shop that would provide income for the couple after Mr. Johnson's retirement.

As part of her research, Ms. Johnson worked for six months as a salesperson at a highly successful antiques mall in a nearby town. This experience gave her an insight into what customers in her area want to buy and what they will pay.

Ms. Johnson also took several business-related courses through the adult education division of the local college. These courses included instruction in basic business practices, public relations, and advertising.

Ms. Johnson is active in the educational and cultural aspects of the city. Through her shop she will also contribute to the economic well-being of the city as a tax-paying businessperson and by hiring part-time employees. She will join the YourTown Chamber of Commerce, the Better Business Bureau, and Lions International.

Timing of Opening of Sally's Antiques

Most dealers in antiques see a definite trend regarding months of high sales volume and months when sales are low. Statistically, dealers in antiques make their greatest profits during the months between Memorial Day and Christmas. Profits are usually lowest during January and February.

Ms. Johnson will open her shop the first week in March. This will give her time to become established and for the shop to become known in the community before the heavy summer selling season begins.

Location of Sally's Antiques

Sally's Antiques is located in Mr. and Ms. Victor Johnson's home at 123 Oak Drive in a pleasant, residential neighborhood, zoned R2, on the edge of the business district. The zoning laws of YourTown allow small, in-home businesses in this neighborhood.

Oak Drive is three blocks from Main Street, the primary traffic artery in YourTown. Highway Department figures state that approximately 750 cars per day pass along Oak Drive. Traffic on Main Street often averages 1,000 cars per hour. This traffic flow affords excellent visibility for Sally's Antiques.

The shop is about one-half mile from the center of YourTown's business district. Some customers will be able to walk to the shop; most, however, will drive. Parking is allowed on Oak Drive, and there's space for three cars to park in front of the shop.

Oak Drive is within the city limits of YourTown, so it has full police and fire department coverage. There is adequate water and electric service.

An alley at the rear of the property allows Ms. Johnson to unload antiques for sale in the shop and to load those scheduled for delivery to customers.

The Johnson home is large, so there are ample living quarters still available at the rear of the first floor and on the second floor. The original living, dining, and breakfast rooms have been converted into a shop area. The selling area is approximately 600 square feet.

Ms. Johnson plans to have a side porch, which now opens into this area, enclosed in the near future. This enclosure will provide an additional 150 square feet to the shop. A ramp has been constructed along the front steps of the home to make the building wheelchair accessible.

Ms. Johnson will also have sod removed from the front lawn and replaced with blacktop. This will provide three off-street parking places.

The Market for Antiques in YourTown

YourTown now has a vibrant population of approximately 30,000 people. The economic indicators for the town are good.

The fastest-growing segment of the population in YourTown consists of couples between the ages of thirty and forty-five. Most of these couples have children. Many of these men and women are employed at the local engineering plant, which is expanding its work force and expects a 15 percent increase in personnel within the next three years.

The median family income of professional employees at the plant is $60,000, and 74 percent of these couples have college degrees. These people are in a financial position to buy quality antiques, but not those with extremely high price tags. Ms. Johnson plans to tap this large and growing market by carrying primarily antiques in the middle-price range.

Competition for Sally's Antiques

Three antiques shops already exist in YourTown. One shop specializes in fine antiques that are quite expensive. This shop does not appear to be especially successful.

Another shop carries a variety of antiques, but most are in the lower-price range and can only be described as collectibles. Because this shop is overly crowded and frequently dusty, it resembles a flea market. Most of its customers are shopping for bargain-basement merchandise.

The third shop carries a good selection of antiques in all price ranges. This shop appears to be quite successful. In addition, a large antiques mall opened recently in a shopping mall at the edge of town. This mall draws customers from a wide area.

Statistically, a town of 30,000 can easily support several antiques shops. Since Sally's Antiques has the advantage of being the only home-based shop in town, is centrally located, and also appeals primarily to middle-income buyers, the prognosis for its success is good.

Because Ms. Johnson will display her antiques in a homelike setting, her customers will be able to visualize them in their own homes.

Projections for Financial Success

Ms. Johnson researched the success potential for her shop on two levels: (1) national and (2) local.

1. She found four articles in national business-oriented magazines that discussed the current economic health of antiques shops throughout the United States. Here is the gist of those articles:
   • Overall, income in antiques shops has been consistent with small-business income in general except for the last two years during a national

recession, from 2001 to 2003. Statistics show a dramatic slump in sales during the first part of that period but an increase in high end sales toward the end due to more investment in antiques.

• Twelve national magazines devoted to either women's issues or decorating regularly feature photographs of attractive homes that contain antiques. This creates a desire among homemakers to use antiques in their homes too.

• The number of antiques shops, nationwide, increased 25 percent from 1990 to 2000, with the highest number of antique collectors born in the 1950s and 1960s. However, the number of people in their 30s and 40s is the highest, therefore indicating a continuing growing market for antiques.

2. Ms. Johnson talked with the owners of three antiques shops in YourTown and two shop owners in a nearby city. One of the shop owners planned to close his store within two months as he was not making a profit. His problem appeared to be one of poor management, based on little or no advertising and an unattractive and dingy shop interior. One shop owner said he was breaking even, but not showing much profit. Apparently, he had been in the antiques business in another part of the country prior to moving to YourTown and had not realized the difference in customer demand between the two areas. The other owners, all of whom had been in business a minimum of three years, claimed to be making a decent living from their shops.

Analysis of Potential Problems

Ms. Johnson analyzed her personal lifestyle and the business practices of other antiques shops in YourTown and determined she has two main problems to overcome:

1. Keeping the shop open six days a week throughout the year would mean no time for a vacation or visits to children and grandchildren in other cities. She decided, therefore, that she would contract with a local temporary employment agency and hire a salesperson to work in the shop for three weeks every winter during the slow season.

2. Since her shop is the newest in YourTown, she'll have to do extensive public relations work in the community to let people know of it and to establish a following. Toward this end, she'll offer to speak at various clubs and service organizations, giving information about understanding and collecting antiques. She'll approach the continuing education department of the local community college and propose a short course in the same topics. She'll have flyers printed advertising her shop and distribute them in local hotels, motels, and bed-and-breakfast inns. She'll contact local interior decorators and invite them to a private wine-and-cheese party in the shop to acquaint them with her inventory.

Short- and Long-term Goals

Short-term goals for the shop (one year) are to reach the break-even point within six months, create a mailing list of 300 customers, and increase inventory by approximately 10 percent a month.

Long-term goals—two to five years—are to enlarge the selling area and to create off-street parking. Ms. Johnson also plans to begin making annual buying trips to the Midwest and Northeast to enhance the variety and quality of the antiques she carries.

Her overall goal in opening and operating Sally's Antiques is to provide a substantial income to supplement Mr. Johnson's retirement pension.

Business Structure

Ms. Johnson will own and operate the shop as sole proprietor. Although Mr. Johnson will assist her in some aspects of managing the shop, her attorney advised her to retain ownership in her own name.

Professional Counselors

Ms. Johnson has acquired the services of several local professionals to assist her in various legal and financial matters:

1. Carol Collins, attorney
2. William Seward, Certified Public Accountant
3. Helen Danforth, Central Insurance Agency
4. Roland Prospect, Vice President, First Bank

Each of these professionals has set up a system for the business based on his or her own specialty.

Advertising and Promotion Strategy

Ms. Johnson is allotting 3 percent of her budget for advertising during the first year of operation to gain high visibility for the shop. This percentage will drop to 2 percent in the second year.

Most of this money will be spent on print advertising in the local newspaper, the *Register*. She will run large display ads for two weeks prior to her grand opening, then small classified ads weekly after that.

Ms. Johnson has arranged with the newspaper for a discounted rate on regular classified ads. She will run a 3-inch, one-column ad every week, spotlighting different antiques each time.

Ms. Johnson will run spot announcements of the grand opening on a local radio station, KABC, in the week prior to the grand opening.

Ms. Johnson will also schedule regular promotional activities throughout the year. These will include two annual sales, on-site talks by a local historian, a costume contest, display of especially valuable antiques, and so forth. These promotions will be announced through press releases to all local media. The two annual sales will be announced through mailings to previous customers.

Pricing and Service Strategies

Because Sally's Antiques is home-based, Ms. Johnson has a lower overhead for the shop than do her competitors. The shop comprises approximately 20 percent of the total square footage of the home, so she is able to deduct 20 percent of what she pays on her mortgage, on her taxes, and for utilities. This savings allows Ms. Johnson to sell comparable antiques at a slightly lower price than do other shops in town.

Mr. and Ms. Johnson own a 2002 Ford van, which they will use to haul antiques to the shop and to deliver purchased antiques to customers. They will deliver any antique with a purchase price of $200 or more free of charge within a 10-mile radius of YourTown's city limits. Ms. Johnson will add a surcharge of $10 for delivery of any antique priced at less than $200. Mr. Johnson will drive the truck for these deliveries.

For customers who live at a greater distance, Ms. Johnson will arrange for delivery through a local moving company.

Ms. Johnson will accept credit cards. She will place antiques on layaway with a nonrefundable 30 percent down payment, the balance to be paid off within three months.

Financial Data

Ms. Johnson had approximately $20,000 in ready cash and savings when she began the process of adapting her home to become a shop. Approximately $12,500 of these funds will be used to remodel her home and for start-up expenses.

Approximate Projected Start-up Costs

Remove one partition to enlarge selling area	$ 500
Remove carpeting	150
Refinish hardwood floors	500
Upgrade existing electrical wiring	850
New light fixtures	300
New drywall and trim (installed)	650
Repaint two interior walls and trim	500
New window coverings	325
Shelving	650
Exterior sign	300
Exterior painting	1,500
Landscaping	800
Office supplies	300
Computer	1,100
Business cards	75
Business telephone line	125
Yellow Pages ad (one month)	125
Answering machine	50
Business checks	45
Subscriptions to trade journals, price guides	225
Business memberships	125
Business license	25
Initial attorney and CPA fees	500
Insurance (shop and truck annually)	1,500
Advertising (grand opening)	500
Labor (minimum wage)	800
Total projected start-up costs	$12,520

Ms. Johnson should have approximately $7,480 in cash as a reserve after paying for these start-up costs.

Ms. Johnson had been buying and storing antiques for about two years prior to the opening of the shop. These antiques make up her initial inventory. Their market value is approximately $5,000.

Ms. Johnson expects to break even in the shop within six months. Prior to that time she's aware that her expenses (pro-rated for the shop space in the home) for utilities and mortgage payments, plus advertising, attorney and CPA fees, and insurance will undoubtedly exceed her cash income. Based on her research of other shops in the area, she expects to begin making a profit of approximately $500 the sixth month, with steadily increasing amounts in the following months. She expects to be clearing approximately $1,500 a month by the end of her first year in business.

Personal Income Statement

Mr. and Ms. Johnson own their own home in YourTown. The current value of the home is approximately $210,000. They have an equity of approximately $65,000 in the home, and their mortgage payments, based on a fixed 6.25 percent loan, are $620 per month.

The Johnsons own two vehicles, a 1997 Honda Civic and a 2002 Ford van. The Honda is free and clear of a loan, but payments on the van are $350 per month. They have no other outstanding debts.

The couple has a fixed income of $1,585 per month. Mr. Johnson receives a Social Security payment of $750 per month and a company pension of $835 per month. This income is sufficient for the couple's personal expenses.

As I mentioned earlier in this chapter, this detailed business plan is primarily for your own use to help you foresee and work your way through all the details of opening your shop. Should you, in a year or two, find the need for a bank loan, you'll need to write a different, greatly condensed business plan to present to your potential lender. As one Small Business Administration counselor says, "Most lenders, at first, are not interested in all the details of how you run your business. They just want the bare facts to determine if you're a good risk. If they decide to pursue your application further, they'll ask for balance sheets, IRS forms, and so forth."

Chapter Four
Keeping Records

Most antiques dealers aren't really numbers-type people. Their joy comes from the pleasure of working with objects that brought beauty or employment or service to men and women many generations ago. They love the patina on an old table, where a few nicks chart the thousands of meals served to loving families. Morning sunlight blazing through cut glass is as bewitching to them as diamonds. An old hand-tied Persian rug, though faded and worn, is, to them, an object of rare beauty.

Sound familiar? Most don't really relish the chore of scribbling numbers in little squares. It's boring. It's frustrating. It's time-consuming. Who needs bookkeeping? As with many other facets of life, once you try it, it isn't nearly as frightening as it seemed at first.

One definition of bookkeeping is "the recording of financial data, income, and expenditures that relate to your business." This information will come from sales receipts of antiques you sell, from receipts of things you buy or services you pay for, and from your check register. (Now, that's not so scary, is it?)

Good records make it easy to see where your money is going and whether you're spending it wisely. Have you done too much advertising or too little? Are your insurance premiums too high for your budget or is more insurance needed? Is money available now for that computer package you've been eyeing, or should you wait a couple of more months? Did the Christmas sale bring in as much income as your spring sale?

With good records it's easy to see when you bought each antique, how much you paid for it, when you sold it, and how much gross profit you made on its sale. Just as important, when you keep accurate and complete records, your accountant will make sure you take every legal deduction allowed by the IRS. This can mean a substantial lowering of your tax bill come April 15 each year.

Keep the IRS Happy

Another consideration is that the IRS looks closely at the records of all home-based businesses. If you don't have good records of your expenditures and income, the IRS could well say you're running your shop not as a business but as a hobby. Then all your deductions would be disallowed and you'd have to pay a whopping tax bill.

I'll grant you that it's a whole lot more fun to be out scouting for antiques or showing them to customers than keeping books. If you want to make a profit in this business, however, you need to spend a few minutes every day putting some numbers in little squares. Most home-based antiques dealers can complete all the bookkeeping for the average shop in half an hour a day, plus two or three hours wrapping up at the end of the month. In all honesty, once you get the hang of how to keep a ledger, it's really not as bad as it seems— *just take it one step at a time.*

Fortunately, owners of home-based antiques shops don't have to maintain complicated records. Buying and selling practices are far simpler than those of most retailers, so bookkeeping is simpler too. Most dealers just set a certain time of day, maybe early morning when few customers are expected, to update the ledger.

It's a good idea to get some basic instruction in bookkeeping. These skills will make keeping records, once you understand the system, an easy task. Afterwards you should be able to manage your daily record keeping on your own.

You can also hire a professional bookkeeping service to handle this task if you like. In this case, you would need to file all receipts for purchases you make, sales receipts for sales in the shop, canceled checks you've written, and so forth, in separate folders, then let the bookkeeper record those figures in the ledgers. The bookkeeper can come to your shop to pick up the data, or you can drop it off at her office. Either way, the information is input into a computer and formatted properly and accurately for your accountant. This is a reasonable alternative for dealers who simply don't want to handle the bookkeeping end of their business.

The biggest disadvantage of hiring an outside bookkeeping service is that you lose control over your records. The bookkeeper knows where all your money is going or coming from, but unless you spend a great deal of time analyzing the printouts she hands you, you won't have the foggiest notion of what the totals mean. Remember that you will have the bookkeeper's monthly service fee to pay, even during those first months in business when income may be spotty. The bookkeeper, too, cannot figure your taxes or advise you about management of the business. This task remains with your accountant. Regardless of whether you do your own books or hire a bookkeeping service, though, your accountant should be in on the system right from the very beginning.

A record-keeping system that's right for you and your shop will encompass the following criteria:

- It will be easy to learn and understand.
- It will be easy to maintain.
- It will foster accuracy.
- It will encourage timely entries.
- It will be complete.

At any office supply store you can find several prepackaged commercial bookkeeping systems that fulfill these needs.

If you are quite comfortable with computers, you can certainly use any one of several excellent software systems to keep your records. They aren't expensive, and once you get the hang of them, they're easy to use. Ask your accountant to recommend one.

See page 96 for information about computer software that can make your bookkeeping easier.

The following information is for those of you who prefer to keep your records in a ledger.

Remember the K.I.S.S. Principle
(Keep It Simple, Stupid)

As you peruse the ledgers offered you, look first and foremost for *simplicity*. Their chart of accounts should have predesignated categories that can be easily adapted to your needs. As you study the various systems, ask yourself these questions: Will I find it simple to transfer my daily income to a balance at the end of the month? Can I tell at a glance how much my monthly income exceeds my expenses or vice versa?

Whichever system you choose, be sure it's based on *single-entry bookkeeping*. These are the easiest to use and are quite adequate for a small- to average-size home-based antiques shop. With a single-entry system, you record each transaction only once. You would, for example, record the payment of your gas bill once in a column headed "Heat." A payment for repairs to your truck would be recorded once under "Auto Expense." Even the IRS approves single-entry bookkeeping for small businesses, saying, "This system can be used to record income and expenses *adequately for tax purposes.*"

You will hear another term, *double-entry,* used by bookkeepers and accountants. Double-entry bookkeeping requires you to record each transaction in two separate categories. This system does have the advantage of catching errors, but it's more time-consuming than single-entry bookkeeping and is far more difficult to manage for anyone who didn't make straight A's in Accounting 101!

A single-entry system that's exceptionally easy to use is the Dome Simplified Monthly Bookkeeping Record. This ledger is also recommended by some Small Business Development Center counselors. It's designed by a CPA and is published by Dome Publishing Company. The book usually sells for under $15 at office supply stores, or call the company at (800) 432–4352, or see www.domeproducts.com.

For the person relatively new to business, some of the most valuable pages in this ledger are the three that list some 400 legal deductions the IRS allows small businesses. Did you know, for instance, that you can deduct the cost of Christmas presents you give temporary employees or the value of a Haviland plate your cat knocked off a shelf as she settled in for her midmorning nap?

The Chart of Accounts

Your records will be based on what accountants term a *chart of accounts.* Don't panic. A chart of accounts is simply a general list of your income and expenses in running the shop.

In the Dome ledger your expenses will be listed on a sheet headed "Detail of Monthly Expenditures." Since you're in the retail business, you'll separate your purchases into two categories, the first for antiques you buy for resale, on the left side of the page; and the second for nonmerchandise purchases or expenses, on the right side of the page. (See pages 88–89.)

Every category of expenses in the second group has a predesignated account number. That account number will correspond to an identical code number in your monthly tally of those expenses (see pages 90–91).

The chart on pages 82–83 illustrates a typical commercial chart of accounts, along with its account numbers. The preprinted categories on this sheet are standard ones, formatted to cover the expenses of almost any small business. There is another copy of the chart in the appendix.

Assuming you wanted to use this form, you could record your expenses as follows:

Deductible Expenses

1. *Merchandise and materials.* These are the antiques you buy for resale.
2. *Accounting.* Most businesspeople like to meet with their accountants regularly. It's one good way to make sure that you're on the right track with your own bookkeeping and that you're keeping expenses in line.
3. *Advertising.* Here you'd list expenses for newspaper and radio advertising, cards to customers announcing special promotions, and so forth. If you advertise in the Yellow Pages, that expense goes here, not under Telephone.
4. *Auto.* You will use your car or truck to cruise the yard sales and to visit auctions. All costs in operating those vehicles are entered here, including repairs, tires, and minor purchases such as windshield wipers, tune-ups, and oil changes. Keep a separate log of your mileage in operating the vehicles for business. Don't include a major purchase, such as a truck, here. This is a depreciable expense, which your accountant will record elsewhere.

Chart of Accounts

EXPENDITURES

ACCT NO.	ACCOUNT	TOTAL THIS MONTH	TOTAL UP TO THIS MONTH	TOTAL TO DATE
	DEDUCTIBLE			
1	MDSE. - MATERIALS			
2	ACCOUNTING			
3	ADVERTISING			
4	AUTO EXPENSE			
5	CARTONS, ETC.			
6	CONTRIBUTIONS			
7	DELIVERY EXP.			
8	ELECTRICITY			
9	ENTERTAINMENT			
10	FREIGHT AND EXPR.			
11	HEAT			
12	INSURANCE			
13	INTEREST			
14	LAUNDRY			
15	LEGAL EXPENSE			
16	LICENSES			
17	MISC. EXP.			
18	OFFICE EXP.			
19	POSTAGE			
20	RENT			

TOTAL RECEIPTS FROM BUSINESS OR PROFESSION

DAY		AMOUNT
1		
2		
3		
4		
5		
6		
7		
8		
9		
10		
11		
12		
13		
14		
15		
16		
17		
18		
19		

21	REPAIRS
22	TAX-SALES
23	TAX-SOC. SEC./MED.
24	TAX-STATE U.I.
25	TAX-OTHER
26	SELLING EXP.
27	SUPPLIES
28	TELEPHONE
29	TRADE DUES, ETC.
30	TRAVELING EXP.
31	WAGES AND COMM.
32	WATER

SUB-TOTAL

NON-DEDUCTIBLE

51	NOTES PAYABLE
52	FEDERAL INC. TAX
53	LOANS PAYABLE
54	LOANS RECEIVABLE
55	PERSONAL
56	FIXED ASSETS

TOTAL THIS MONTH

TOTAL UP TO THIS MONTH

TOTAL TO DATE

TOTAL THIS MONTH

TOTAL UP TO THIS MONTH

TOTAL TO DATE

5. *Cartons, shipping expenses, and so forth.* Most small antiques shops don't package or ship their customers' purchases. You may choose to provide this service if your shop is in an area where tourists, who can't take purchases with them, constitute a large part of your business.

6. *Contributions.* As a businessperson, you will inevitably be asked to contribute to community charities and events.

7. *Delivery expenses.* You may decide to deliver some antiques without charging your customers for the service. This is a deductible expense for you.

8. *Electricity.* You will probably pay only one electric bill, one that covers your entire home and shop. The prorated portion of that bill, based on the amount of square footage in your shop, is entered here.

9. *Entertainment.* Most of the dealers I know entertain their customers with good conversation and perhaps a cup of tea on a rainy afternoon. Why not change this category to one you use regularly or ignore it all together?

10. *Freight and express.* Will you go on buying trips and ship some of the antiques back home by freight? Many dealers do this.

11. *Heat.* If you heat your home/shop with any fuel other than electricity, prorate the expense as mentioned in item 8.

12. *Insurance.* Your monthly or quarterly payments for liability, fire and theft, and any other insurance directly related to the business belong here. Do not include premiums for life insurance or other personal insurance.

13. *Interest.* You may someday take out a business loan for expansion or another business expense. The interest on that loan is deductible. Do not include here interest on any personal loans.

14. *Laundry.* No, you can't sell the old Maytag and start sending your sheets and towels to the local laundry and claim that as a business expense. You may, however, want to have your shop curtains laundered or the carpet cleaned by a commercial firm.

15. *Legal expenses.* You will have some attorney expenses when you set up the structure for your shop. You will probably want to pay a brief visit to your attorney every year, too, just for an annual checkup. Do not include here any legal expenses for nonbusiness purposes.

trade newspapers and magazines read by everyone in the antiques business. You'll also have to buy the annual price guides that all dealers rely on.

30. *Travel.* You're allowed to deduct most expenses incurred attending out-of-town antiques shows or on buying trips. This includes meals, motels, taxis, and so forth. However, the IRS does impose some restrictions. Talk with your accountant.

31. *Wages and commissions.* Do you pay wages to an employee? Payments to a temporary employment agency would also be entered here.

32. *Water.* Most cities include water service along with the electric bill. If yours is separate, though, put it here.

33. This number is left blank for any deductible expense not covered above.

34. As with item 33.

35. As with item 33.

ondeductible Expenses

51. *Notes payable.* Did you pay off a personal note?

52. *Federal income tax.* Sorry, this isn't a deductible expense.

53. *Loans payable.* Enter here any payment on a bank or personal loan.

54. *Loans receivable.* Did you lend money to anyone? If the loan is partially or wholly repaid, enter the amount here.

55. *Personal.* This is for your owner's withdrawal (your salary).

56. *Fixed assets.* Will you buy a computer, a new truck, or some other depreciable asset? Enter the cost here.

57. This number is left blank for any nondeductible expense not covered above.

suggest that you don't add too many unusual categories to this list. You might hire a otographer to take a photograph of your shop for a grand opening advertisement, but y have a separate category for "Photography" when you may not hire him again for more an a year? Just enter his charges under "Advertising." You and your accountant can always sert extra categories in your chart of accounts as time goes on, if you find you need them.

16. *Licenses.* You'll have to pay for licenses and permits when you ope
    In addition, you will undoubtedly be assessed annual fees to renew
    license and any others your state requires.
17. *Miscellaneous.* Put here any expense that doesn't seem to fall readily
    category.
18. *Office supplies.* This can be a catchall for bags, price tags, sales b
    forth.
19. *Postage.* Any postage you must use for business purposes goes here
20. *Rent (or mortgage).* Your accountant will determine how much of
    mortgage payments are deductible as a business expense, based o
    footage of your shop. Delete this category if you own your home c
21. *Repairs.* This category would include whatever you have to spend
    building in good condition. Suppose some roof shingles blow
    windstorm. Your expenses in having them replaced would be ente
22. *Sales tax.* If you live in a city, county, or state that charges sales ta
    to charge your customers tax on all sales and send that money to t
    ate agency.
23. *Social Security and Medicare.* You're liable for these taxes only if
    employee. Check with your accountant.
24. *Tax—state unemployment insurance.* See item 23.
25. *Tax—other.* Any other taxes for which you are liable are entered h
26. *Selling expenses.* This is a vague category that includes any expense
    promoting sales in your shop. One example might be gift certificat
    during a special promotion. The only catch here is that the IR!
    expenses to $25 per customer.
27. *Supplies.* You'll need brooms, mops, soaps, and so on, to keep th
    You'll also need brass polishes, ammonia, paper towels, furnitur
    other agents for getting and keeping your antiques in salable cond
28. *Telephone.* Do you have a separate telephone line for the shop?
    charges here. Do not include your household telephone bill.
29. *Trade association dues and subscriptions.* You may join the chamber
    or a service club and have to pay dues. You'll want to subscribe t

None of these categories is written in concrete, however. Every business is different and has different expenses. Should you decide to use this chart of accounts, feel free to adapt it in any way that will suit your shop.

Now take a look at the chart of accounts on pages 90–91. As you'll see, I've made entries on the form to reflect the expenses and income of a small home-based antiques shop.

The chart on pages 88–89 is a register of monthly expenses. The left side of the register records antiques bought for resale. The right side records nonmerchandise expenses, using the account numbers described beginning on page 81. These hypothetical entries are similar to those you might have in your own business. A blank form is in the appendix for you to photocopy.

You'll notice an entry for "Cash purchases" on the merchandise register. Many times you'll have to pay cash for the antiques you buy at yard sales. You won't have any receipts for these sales, so keep a small notebook in your car and record each purchase with a description of the item and the amount paid for it. (This record will come in handy later on, when you price the item.) At the end of the month, total all cash purchases for antiques and enter that figure on the register as "Cash purchases." Then write a company check to yourself to cover the amount.

To put some of the entries on the nonmerchandise side of the chart in perspective, let's suppose you plan to hold a sale in April to generate business after the winter slump. Your biggest expense will be postcards sent to everyone on your mailing list. You buy one hundred stamped postcards at the post office for $25, which you paid for with check #195, then have a copy center print your message on the cards. The copy center charges you $35, which you pay with check #199. You enter the postcards under Postage, category 19, and the printing under Advertising, category 3.

A few days later you take a half hour off to pay some bills. You write check #205 for $23 to the ABC Electric Company and enter it in category 8, Electricity. You write check #206 for $14 to the XYZ Gas Company. This you enter under category 11, Heat.

You also order a copy of one of the new antiques price guides and send your check #207 for $12.95 along with your order. This is a publication and is entered in category 29.

At the end of the month, you transfer these entries to a sheet (see pages 90–91) that records your total expenditures for the month. These totaled expenditures are registered on the right side of the chart.

Detail of Monthly Expenditures

MDSE AND MATERIALS PAID BY CASH AND CHECKS

DAY	TO WHOM PAID	CHECK NO.	AMOUNT
1			
2			
3	Red Barn Auction		78 00
4	Cash purchases		19 10
5	Cash purchases		43 15
6	SLI Estate Sales		18 00
7			
8			
9			
10	Red Barn Auction		24 50
11	Jim Monty (yard sale)		13 05
12	Cash purchases		6 25
13			
14	R.C. Carry Misc. Lot		150 00
15			
16			
17	Red Barn Auction		13 50

OTHER EXPENDITURES BY CHECKS AND CASH

DAY	TO WHOM PAID	CHECK NO.	ACCT. NO.	AMOUNT
1	Post Office	195	19	20 00
2	Happy Home Mortg. Co.	196	20	150 00
3	Kmart	197	27	7 95
3	St. Mary's School	198	6	10 00
4	Rapid Copy Center	199	3	35 00
4	Amer. Lung Assoc.	200	6	15 00
5	Office Depot	201	18	15 00
5	City Brick Co. (walkway)	202	21	60 00
6	Williams Glass Co.	203	21	7 00
6	Register	204	3	25 00
7	ABC Electric	205	8	23 00
7	XYZ Gas Co.	206	11	14 00
7	Schroeder's	207	29	12 95
15	Sam's Auto	208	4	16 95
15	US West Com.	209	28	34 00

Left page

Day	Description	Amount
18	Cash purchases	7 25
18	Indy Land (yard sale)	12 75
19	Cash purchases	3 00
20		
21		
22		
23	Maria Dalhy wicker set	95 00
24		
25		
26	Cash purchases	4 50
27	Tom Kendall Misc. Lot	200 00
28		
29		
30		
31	Carried Forward	688 05

Right page

Day	Account	Check No.			
17	James Accounting	210	2	75	00
21	Kmart	211	18	5	95
21	Chamber of Commerce	212	29	50	00
28	State Farm Ins.	213	12	176	00
30	Aamco Service Station	214	7	12	00
	Carried Forward			765	40

Total Monthly Expenditures

TOTAL RECEIPTS FROM BUSINESS OR PROFESSION

DAY	AMOUNT
1 Closed	
2	174 00
3	95 00
4 (rain)	32 00
5	98 00
6	259 00
7 closed	
8 closed	
9	71 00
10	29 00
11	42 00
12	69 00
13	185 00
14 closed	
15 closed	
16 (sale)	421 00

EXPENDITURES

ACCT NO.	ACCOUNT	TOTAL THIS MONTH	TOTAL UP TO THIS MONTH	TOTAL TO DATE
	DEDUCTIBLE			
1	MDSE.-MATERIALS	688 05	972 20	1660 25 9
2	ACCOUNTING	75 00	225 00	300 00
3	ADVERTISING	60 00	75 00	135 00
4	AUTO EXPENSE	16 95		16 95
5	CARTONS, ETC.			
6	CONTRIBUTIONS	25 00		25 00
7	DELIVERY EXP.	12 00	35 00	47 00
8	ELECTRICITY	23 00	87 00	110 00
9	ENTERTAINMENT			
10	FREIGHT AND EXPR.			
11	HEAT	14 00	59 00	73 00
12	INSURANCE	176 00	176 00	352 00
13	INTEREST			
14	LAUNDRY		39 00	39 00
15	LEGAL EXPENSE			
16	LICENSES			
17	MISC. EXP.		4 50	4 50
18	OFFICE EXP.	20 95	19 00	39 95
19	POSTAGE	20 00		
20	RENT	150 00	450 00	600 00

Left Section

Day	Note	Amount	
17		290 00	
18		98 00	
19	(rain)	15 00	
20	(rain)	29 00	
21	closed		
22	closed		
23		49 00	
24		88 00	
25		105 00	
26	(rain)	42 00	
27		176 00	
28	closed		
29	closed		
30			329 00
31			
TOTAL THIS MONTH			2696 00
TOTAL UP TO THIS MONTH			6975 00
TOTAL TO DATE			9671 00
Memo			

Right Section

	Category	This Month	Up To This Month	Total To Date
21	REPAIRS	67 00		67 00
22	TAX-SALES			
23	TAX-SOC. SEC. / MED.			
24	TAX-STATE U. I.			
25	TAX-OTHER			
26	SELLING EXP.			
27	SUPPLIES	7 95		7 95
28	TELEPHONE	34 60	95 80	138 40
29	TRADE DUES, ETC.	62 95	50 00	112 95
30	TRAVELING EXP.			
31	WAGES AND COMM.		500 00	500 00
32	WATER			
	SUB-TOTAL	1453 45	2787 50	4228 95
	NON-DEDUCTIBLE			
51	NOTES PAYABLE			
52	FEDERAL INC. TAX	150 00	150 00	300 00
53	LOANS PAYABLE			
54	LOANS RECEIVABLE			
55	PERSONAL	1000 00	3000 00	4000 00
56	FIXED ASSETS			
	TOTAL THIS MONTH	2603 45		
	TOTAL UP TO THIS MONTH		5937 50	
	TOTAL TO DATE			8528 95

For Your Tax Adviser—Detachable Summary Sheet

YEAR ENDED 20_____ $_____

CASH RECEIPTS FOR THE YEAR

Accounts Receivable: *Accounts Payable:*   *Inventory*

January 1, 20___ $_____   January 1, 20___ $_____   January 1, 20___ $_____

December 31, 20___ $_____   December 31, 20___ $_____   December 31, 20___ $_____

EQUIPMENT RECORD:

(Equipment Purchased)

Date Acquired M/D/Y	Description	New or Used	Cost or Basis	Life Years	%	Annual Depreciation

(Equipment Sold)

Date Sold M/D/Y	Description	Sales Price or Trade-In	Date Purch. M/D/Y	Accum. Depr.	Remain. Cost or Basis	Gain or Loss

OTHER INFORMATION:

Name of Proprietor _____   Soc. Sec. # _____

Main Business Activity _____   Product _____

Business Name _____   Bus. Address _____

Employer Identification Number _____

Accounting Method: (1) Cash   (2) Accrual   (3) Other _____

Method(s) used to value closing inventory: (1) Cost   (2) Lower of cost or market

(3) Other _____

EXPENDITURES

ACCT. NO.	ACCOUNT	TOTAL FOR YEAR
	DEDUCTIBLE	
1	MDSE.–MATERIALS	
2	ACCOUNTING	
3	ADVERTISING	
4	AUTO EXPENSE	
5	CARTONS, ETC.	
6	CONTRIBUTIONS	
7	DELIVERY EXP.	
8	ELECTRICITY	
9	ENTERTAINMENT	
10	FREIGHT AND EXPR.	
11	HEAT	
12	INSURANCE	
13	INTEREST	
14	LAUNDRY	
15	LEGAL EXPENSE	
16	LICENSES	
17	MISC. EXP.	
18	OFFICE EXP.	
19	POSTAGE	

20	RENT		
21	REPAIRS		
22	TAX-SALES		
23	TAX-SOC. SEC. / MED.		
24	TAX-STATE U. I.		
25	TAX-OTHER		
26	SELLING EXP.		
27	SUPPLIES		
28	TELEPHONE		
29	TRADE DUES, ETC.		
30	TRAVELING EXP.		
31	WAGES AND COMM.		
32	WATER		
	SUB-TOTAL		
	NON-DEDUCTIBLE		
51	NOTES PAYABLE		
52	FEDERAL INC. TAX		
53	LOANS PAYABLE		
54	LOANS RECEIVABLE		
55	PERSONAL		
56	FIXED ASSETS		
	TOTAL FOR YEAR		

Was there any change in determining quantities, cost, or valuations between

opening and closing inventory? Yes_____ No_____

Did you deduct expenses for an office in your home? Yes_____ No_____

Do you have evidence for all listed property (autos, etc.)

to support your deduction? Yes_____ No_____

Is the evidence written? Yes_____ No_____

Record-Keeping Rules for
Business and Entertainment Expenses in General

Adequate records (a log) are required to substantiate:

(1) the business use of "listed property" (i.e., passenger cars or other property used in transportation, property of the type generally used for entertainment, recreation or amusement, computers or peripheral equipment),

(2) traveling expenses, including meals and lodging away from home,

(3) entertainment expenses,

(4) business gifts.

Meals and entertainment must be directly related and have a clear business purpose. Also deductibility is subject to limitation.

IMPORTANT

NO DEDUCTION FOR TRAVEL, ENTERTAINMENT, AUTOMOBILE EXPENSES, ETC., WILL BE ALLOWED UNLESS ADEQUATE RECORDS (A LOG) ARE KEPT.

NO PROOF—NO DEDUCTION

The left side of the chart on pages 90–91 is for registering your income. You list there, every day, your total receipts for that day—not each individual sale, just the total amount. At the end of the month, you add those figures and enter the total at the bottom of the sheet.

In the receipts section you'll enter only *actual cash or checks received,* not money that's still due you. If you sell an antique for $300 and the customer puts it on layaway with a $100 down payment, for instance, you include $100 on the day she gives you that check. When she makes a second payment of $100, you enter $100. When she makes the final payment of $100, you enter that figure.

After you complete each month's records on these sheets, you'll carry the totals forward to identical sheets on which you record your expenses and income for the following month. (The chart on pages 90–91 shows figures carried forward from previous months.) This pattern continues until the end of the year. Each month you'll have a record of expenses and income for that month, along with a total of expenses and income for the year to date.

At the end of the year, you'll transfer the final totals to a sheet that you'll give to your accountant (see pages 92–93). With this information, she can quickly and accurately prepare your profit and loss statement and your IRS forms.

Spend a few minutes studying these charts, and you'll see how simple good record keeping can be. But please remember that this is only a hypothetical example of a chart of accounts. You and your accountant can adjust this example to suit your own situation.

As time goes on you'll see how practical and useful this information can be. The income record, for example, will show you at a glance which days, weeks, and months of the year are the most profitable for you. This information can be highly valuable as you plan your merchandising schedule.

Let's say you decided at first to stay open Monday through Saturday. Yet you see, after studying your income register for several months, that you have few sales on Mondays. You just might choose to close the doors on Mondays, save on the electric bill, and go fishing!

You may discover that you make many more sales during the first two weeks of the month than during the last two. Some dealers attribute this phenomenon to the fact that many people are paid on the last Friday of the month. By the middle of the following month, they're running out of discretionary cash. If your record shows this to be true for your shop, you'd know to hold any special sales during the first week of the month, when your customers' wallets are fatter.

Are sales way down the first month or two of the year? Then call your travel agent and book your vacation to Bali for next January!

One hint about paying your utility bills: You may find that your income is too low in certain months, especially during the winter, to cover the high utility bills most of us receive then. You can help your cash flow during this period by arranging for a budget plan with your utilities company in which they bill you the same amount every month throughout the year. In this way you'll be able to budget for your bill, which will be the same in February as in August.

Keep an Orderly Filing System

A file a day keeps the panic away. You need to have some sort of order in your filing system to be able to record the entries in your chart of accounts quickly and efficiently. Just buy a few file folders at an office supply store. Label one "Accounts Payable" and drop all bills into it as they arrive. Label another "Accounts Paid" and drop the invoices there after you've paid them. If you're doing any outside work such as setting up estate sales, label one file folder "Accounts Receivable" and place copies of the invoices you've sent to your clients in it. Once you get the checks for those services, place the invoices in a file labeled "Invoices Paid."

Reconcile your accounts every month *without fail*. Buy a small check file that separates your canceled checks by month. Then if you ever have to prove payment of a bill, you can easily cross-check the paid invoice for that service or merchandise with its corresponding canceled check. Therein lies the road to sanity where record keeping is concerned.

Be sure to deposit all checks and cash you receive for sales in the shop or any other service you perform into your *business checking account*. No fair slipping a check into your personal account to cover that plane ticket to Bali! Most dealers like to make these deposits every evening, leaving enough in the till to make change the next day.

Record Keeping with a Computer

Can a computer make record keeping easier? The answer to this question is a resounding "Maybe!" It all depends on a couple of things:

1. How adept are you at computer technology? If you understand computer language and how to use a spreadsheet and word processing package, then certainly, this is the only way to go.
2. Do you already own a computer and printer? If not, you'd have to spend perhaps $800 to $1,000 for hardware and software to service your bookkeeping needs.

Is a Computer Necessary?

Granted, this is the age of technology, and although everyone from kindergarten-age kids to grandmas is talking bytes and bits, RAM and ROM, not everyone needs a computer. Do you have to use a computer to keep your records? No. As a small-business person managing a shop with minimal bookkeeping requirements, you can do just fine with a few pencils and a ledger. But a computer can save you hours of work each week and perform some amazing tasks.

Bookkeeping Programs

Go down to your computer store and ask to see accounting programs for small businesses. You'll find several on the shelves. The most popular are Quicken and QuickBooks. Both of these programs are user-friendly, but QuickBooks is sufficient for a small business.

What Can a Good Computer Package Do for You?

Once your spreadsheet system is in place, you'll just type the information in and the machine takes over from there. Data about expenses and income will almost automatically land in the right place. A computer can even write checks for your expenses, making paying your bills easy, with virtually no chance of errors. The computer will add columns of figures for you and transfer totals to the proper category. You can give your accountant a printout that's so accurate and complete that she will spend far less time preparing your tax returns and year-end profit and loss statements. Since your accountant charges by the hour, you'll save perhaps hundreds of dollars every year on that bill alone.

Mailing and "Want" Lists. In Chapter 9 you'll find recommendations to keep a mailing list of customers to whom you can send announcements of special promotions. Your word processing package can churn out hundreds of individually addressed letters, cards, and labels that look as though you typed them specifically for that customer. Will you keep a "want list" of antiques for your regular customers? Make a database of those wants and you can almost immediately access any item and who's looking for it.

Let's say one of your customers comes in looking for a collectible Hummel plate as a gift for her sister. You don't have any such plates at that time, so you file her name, telephone number, and the words Hummel plate in your "want list" data file. Three weeks later you locate such a plate, but you can't remember the customer's name. You just go into your "want list" database, tell it to search for Hummel plate, and in seconds you'll see the customer's name and telephone number flashing on the monitor.

Inventory Lists. You'll want to keep an ongoing record of every antique you buy for resale and the price you paid for it. This is the only way you can be sure the price tag you place on the antique reflects a reasonable profit for you. Yes, you can keep such a record in a notebook, but in time, after you've bought thousands of antiques for the shop, that record becomes pretty unwieldy. Make a database for your inventory, though, and the chore is simplicity itself.

It helps to devise a coding system, such as "SS" stands for sterling silver, "J" for jewelry, "G" for glassware, "C" for china, "F" for furniture, "B" for books, "L" for linens, and so forth. Assign sequential numbers to the antiques. For instance, the first piece of jewelry was given the code number "J100," the second piece "J101," the third "J102," and so on. If you use separate sections of the database for each type of antique, this will make it easy to locate any one item, when you bought it, and how much you paid for it.

Say you buy that Hummel plate for $35 and price it at $140. You give it the code number C253 because it's china and happens to be the 253rd piece of china you've placed in the shop. The customer buys the plate on June 21 and asks for the standard 10 percent discount, which you agree to give her. You go into the computer, bring up your "China" file, locate that plate, and record the date of the sale, the dollar amount of the sale, and the percentage of markup you achieved on the sale (more about figuring markup percentages in Chapter 7). You now have a complete record of that purchase and sale. The chart below shows how a page of such entries in the category of china might look. A blank copy of this form is in the appendix of this book.

Sample China File

Code	Item	Cost	Price	Sold At	Date	% Markup
C246	Cookie jar	$1.00	$39	$39	4/13	97%
C247	China bowl	$1.75	$19	$19	2/10	90%
C248	Pitcher	$.95	$12	$10.80	3/23	92%
C249	Delft dish	$3.50	$29	$29	1/30	88%
C250	Creamer	$.25	$6	$5.40	4/23	96%
C251	Salt/pepper	$3	$9	$9	5/18	67%
C252	Cup/saucer	$1	$9	$9	2/28	89%
C253	Xmas plate	$35	$140	$126	6/21	72%
C254	Miniature dish	$.50	$17	$17	7/30	97%
C255	Perfume	$5	$19	$17.10	2/15	71%
C256	Cookie jar	$4	$19	$19	1/15	78%
C257	Bowl/pitcher	$12	$39	$39	3/20	69%
C258	Pitcher	$4	$17	$15.30	2/14	74%

What Kind of Computer Should You Buy?

Should you decide to purchase a computer, your local computer store offers two types of systems: IBM-compatible personal computers, known as PCs, which use Microsoft Windows as their operating system; and Macintosh, known as MACs, which use a different operating system devised by Apple Computers. The majority of businesses use PCs since they cost less and are more cost-efficient. Whichever type you buy, you'll need to get some basic training. Many community colleges offer relatively inexpensive basic computer courses. You might also check with your local library, which may offer courses through a computer club.

As mentioned in Chapter 2, you should consider purchasing a used computer. Now that computers have been around for a few years, larger businesses are upgrading their equipment, and their used machines are going on the market as lease-backs. Unlike in the past, you can buy just about any brand of computer since they've become standardized, much like televisions. However, what you need to investigate is the computer company's customer service should something go wrong. Computer repair can be very expensive, so it pays to check out extended warranty plans, even for used computers. Purchasing one of these plans will give you the peace of mind that, should your system stop working for any reason, you won't be hit with a huge repair bill.

Before you do purchase a computer, new or used, ask your friends and other business-people which ones they use. Recommendations go a long way when buying a computer. Also, you may want to forgo a desktop for a laptop if your space is limited and you plan on carrying your office with you to shows.

Printers. You'll be offered many options in printers too. You don't need to pay for a laser printer. They're fine for offices that require high-quality printing. An ink-jet printer will work fine for your needs. Cartridges for these can be expensive, so it pays to shop the Internet for discount remanufactured cartridges—used cartridges that have not only been refilled but their printing heads cleaned or replaced.

Software. You don't need to buy a lot of software to run an antiques shop. If you purchase a PC, it will usually come with a version of Windows installed. Microsoft Windows contains a lot of programs that can be useful, such as WordPad for basic word processing, Windows Picture Editor for editing digital photographs, computer maintenance programs, and so forth. But you'll also need to buy an office suite package like Microsoft Office, which contains Microsoft Word for word processing; Excel for creating spreadsheets for record keeping; and Access, a database to list your inventory. In addition, you'll also need an accounting package like QuickBooks.

Analyze Your Records for Profit

About twice a year you should take a few hours to analyze all your monthly records. By then you'll be able to see patterns in your sales and expenses that you can use to increase your profit ratio.

Examine Your Expenses

As you study your records, ask yourself three questions about any regular expenses that seem out of line:

1. Why are these expenses high?
2. Is there any way I can reduce them?
3. Should I incur these expenses at all?

Do your fuel and electric bills skyrocket during midwinter months? Maybe you should consider cutting back on your shop hours then, opening an hour later in the morning and closing a half hour earlier in the afternoon. Many antiques shops do this to save money during the slow months. Can you do without some of the office supplies you usually buy? Are you shopping for these supplies at the lowest prices available? Is there any way you can lower expenses on your trips out of town to antiques shows? For example, instead of driving in the night before and staying in a motel, you could get up early and arrive just as the show opens.

Sometimes you don't want to eliminate an expense, but you can look for ways to use it more creatively. Let's take your advertising as an example. Say your original advertising plan calls for a large classified ad in your local newspaper at a certain date each month. If you see from your daily sales record that your greatest sales volume every month is nearly always the few days following the insertion of that ad, you know the money you spend on advertising is paying off in extra income. Those data tell you to increase your advertising budget and schedule additional ads.

If you notice an obvious glitch in your expense records and some item is way too high, take action immediately to lower or eliminate it. You can always refine your method as time goes on.

Examine Your Profit Potential

If you examine your records of the purchase price and selling price of each antique placed in your shop, you'll see clearly where you should be investing your inventory money. Most savvy dealers look at the *ratio* or *percentage* of markup on an item as being just as important as, if not more important than, the actual *dollar* profit.

Take this example. An auctioneer advertised an estate sale that seemed promising, so the antiques dealer arrived bright and early. As the morning wore on, he watched pieces of furniture being sold for fairly good prices. A fine golden oak square side table went for only $75. He didn't bid on it because he knew that the most he could expect to sell it for would be $135, a dollar profit of only $60 on an investment of $75, or a markup of 44 percent. Other dealers didn't bid on that table for the same reason.

But when the auctioneer got to lots of cups and saucers, the dealer, along with most of the others, began bidding. He was able to purchase fourteen different sets for a total of $45. He knew he could easily sell those cups and saucers for an average price of $20 per set, with a total sales price of $280. He would make a dollar profit of $235 on an investment of $45, or a markup of 84 percent. He based his decision to buy the cups and saucers on his inventory records, which showed a *sustained pattern* of making a higher percentage on china than on furniture.

Store Your Records Carefully

Buy what's called a "banker's box" at your office supply store to keep your records and receipts for at least three years. The IRS requires you to keep them for a minimum of three years, but most accountants advise their clients to keep records for six years. It won't hurt, and you just might need them someday if you're ever called in for an audit. Those pesky records will then become your best friends.

Chapter Five
Stocking Your Antiques

Knowing What to Buy and Stock

You'll be investing your good hard cash in the antiques you place in your shop. Obviously, the only way you'll make a profit is if you can sell them, within a reasonable length of time, at a profit. Unless you've been working in another antiques shop recently, you may not know just what your potential customers will want to buy.

A good way to get that information is to select a number of successful antiques shops, both commercial and home-based, in your general area and make a survey of the stock in them. The owners of these shops will carry what their customers want to buy, or they wouldn't stay in business long.

It's easy to believe you know what other dealers are carrying, but you can be misled. When you go into an antiques shop, you drift toward the types of things you like, and you pass right by items you don't. Perhaps you love beautiful marble, for example, so you make a beeline for every marble-topped piece of furniture in every shop you visit. Yet you pass right by most wicker furniture because you don't particularly care for it. It would be very easy for you to believe that shops carry more marble-topped dressers and tables than wicker furniture, because you see the marble and not the wicker. But you'll have to train your mind to know that this isn't the case, since wicker furniture outsells marble at least ten to one.

What this boils down to is that you must open your eyes, ignore your personal preferences, and stock what other people want to buy. There are collectors of virtually every item ever created on this planet, from ice picks to toothpicks. Today, in the back of antiques trade papers, you might find classified ads for old cereal boxes with the cereal still in them, typewriter ribbons in their boxes, or even old firecracker packs.

As you walk through the shops, also make an educated guess about the amount of furniture the owners display in comparison to the china, pottery, glassware, paper goods, and so forth. This will tell you whether they make their greatest profits on furniture or accessories, for they know from experience what sells. You'll know then how to allocate your precious floor and shelf space.

Look carefully at the furniture you do see. How much of it is formal and how much casual primitives? Which woods do you see used most often—walnut, mahogany, oak, pine? That's what their customers ask for and buy.

Do you see many framed prints, mirrors, old photographs? Is Fiesta ware still hot? Do the owners of the shop display much Shelley, Belleek, Limoges? What about fine crystal? Have people in your area jumped on the fifties bandwagon? Does Orientalia seem to be popular?

What about the prices? Do the owners seem to carry antiques in a wide range of prices, or do they specialize in high, low, or moderately priced items?

The chart on page 106 illustrates a form you can use to record this information after you've visited each shop. Make photocopies of it if you need more. Then study the results and keep them in mind as you buy the stock for your own shop.

Where Will You Get Your Stock?

Unless you inherited a three-story house jammed with antiques, you'll have to begin acquiring the inventory for your shop many months before you actually open the doors. You'll need hundreds of items to fill your shelves, cabinets, and floor space. Obviously, you have to buy these antiques at prices that will allow you to cover your expenses and make a profit. Also, each piece you sell must be quickly replaced with another. So, how can you develop a system that will provide you with a continuous, reliable source of antiques at substantial discounts?

The usual places where most other antiques dealers buy their stock are estate sales, auctions, yard sales, individuals (who wish to sell anything from one copper teapot to a truck full of antiques), and other dealers.

Many dealers also go on annual buying trips. Some dealers, especially those who manage their shops alone and don't have time for much scouting on their own, employ a small army of what are known in the business as "pickers." Many dealers take in antiques on consignment. A few create *instant inventory* by buying the entire stock of another dealer who's going out of business.

Estate Sales

An estate sale often occurs when an elderly person dies or goes into a nursing home. The family takes what it wants from the home and hires a *liquidator* to come in, price the rest, then sell it to the public. These liquidators price the goods higher than they would be at a yard sale but lower than what would be charged in an antiques shop. You'll often find excellent-quality antiques at such a sale. I've bought sterling silver, fine sets of china, old prints, quilts, and numerous other antiques at estate sales.

The sale is usually held inside the home on weekends. In some towns local liquidators have quite a following and their sales always draw big crowds. Often when the home where the sale is to be held is small, they'll use a "take a number" system to control the crowds. The first person in line gets number one, the second number two, and so on. If this is the case in your town and you know from advance advertising that a sale appears to be promising, you should plan to arrive long before the starting time to get a low number.

Most liquidators advertise that anything left on Sunday afternoon will be sold at half price. You'll seldom find much of real value left at the end of such sales, but you can usually pick up a few collectibles—linens, kitchenware, and so forth—so you should always go back for one last look.

Auctions

Auctions are a great way to buy antiques—if you bid wisely—and are loads of fun. You'll get some really good laughs just watching the antics of the auctioneers and their helpers.

Consignment Auctions. Consignment auctions are usually held regularly on the same day of the week or month in a large building owned by the auctioneer. Dozens of people may bring merchandise to be sold, and the quality ranges from good to abominable. In

Stock Survey Record

Shop	Furniture	Glassware	China	Other	Prices	Remarks

many cases a great deal of this merchandise is pure junk, even leftover yard-sale stuff.

Antiques dealers attend these auctions faithfully even though individual items to be sold are seldom advertised in advance. The dealers just take their chances on finding quality antiques at this type of auction. You couldn't, for example, attend one with the express purpose of buying an early Victorian bed. Maybe there'll be one there, maybe not.

Estate Auctions. Another type of auction is the estate auction, a one-time-only event held to dispose of the entire contents of a home. The sale is often held on the premises. Auctioneers of these events usually place large display ads in newspapers advertising the sale, and they nearly always include a long list of items to be auctioned. You just might find that Victorian bed on the list, along with hundreds of other antiques.

Buying Procedures at Auctions. Regardless of where an auction is held, the procedure for buying is the same. You approach a table or counter where one or two people sit and ask for a *bidding card.* The person there will ask for some identification, then issue you a large cardboard card that has a number written on it. The card costs nothing, but you can't bid without it.

Smart dealers always arrive at an auction at least a half hour before its advertised starting time. The first reason is to stake out a place up front close to the auctioneer, where it's easy to see the merchandise being auctioned. Most auctioneers will let you reserve such a seat in some way. One method is to tape a piece of paper with your name on it to the seat.

The second reason for arriving early is to look over the merchandise. Many auctioneers won't allow you to browse through the items once the auction starts, and if you haven't scrutinized everything carefully beforehand, you can make some big mistakes once the bidding begins. Few auctioneers are really dishonest, and most will point out a flaw if they know of it, but all merchandise at an auction is sold as is. No returns.

You should walk through the merchandise to be auctioned, taking note of anything you might want to bid on. Examine those pieces carefully for cracks, chips, missing pieces, or any other flaws. Every item will have a lot number, which auctioneers call out when the piece comes up before them. Write the lot number of antiques on which you plan to bid on the back of your bidding card. Beside the number, write the amount you're willing to bid for it, based on what you think you could sell the antique for. Dealers always write the highest bid they're willing to go on every item on the back of the card. This is good insurance against getting caught up in what's called "auction fever."

You bid by holding up your card. If a Wedgwood vase, for example, comes up, the auctioneer will start the bidding by saying, "Who'll give me $500 for this vase?" or some such patter. *Never bid at that first price!* That's just the auctioneer's way of getting the bidding started. He will invariably then say something like, "All right, who'll give me $100?"

If you're new to buying at auctions, I suggest you attend several of them before placing a bid. You can learn a lot about buying at auctions by watching the other dealers.

How do you know who's a dealer? They're the ones constantly checking the back of their bidding card as they bid. They're the ones who look so serious that you'd think they were in the middle of a business conference. They enjoy the auctions, but they don't get emotional about them, as do most bidders who aren't dealers.

Any antiques auction offers the potential for finding good buys, but for real bargains you can't beat the ones held in the country. The farther the auction is from a large town, the better your chances will be to come home with your car full of treasures at rock-bottom prices.

A Virginia dealer was out for a drive on a beautiful fall day, but not out scouting. She stopped at a country store to buy a cold drink and noticed a flyer on the window announcing an auction. Being an auction addict, she asked the store owner how to get there. He told her to go 8 miles down the road and then 5 miles down another road before turning onto a gravel road. So she started out and drove and drove and drove. Pretty soon, she headed farther and farther into the hills. She finally found the place and parked her car. There were quite a few people milling around looking at the merchandise spread out in front of the beautiful country home, but not many dealers, so she was able to make some excellent buys. One of the best was a large cardboard box that held a beautiful silver water pitcher, eight silver dinner plates, three silver trays, and several small silver bowls. They were all salable antiques, for which she paid $5.00 for the box.

Many auctions go on for hours and hours. Plan to stay until the end, because that's often when you'll get your best buys, maybe even some real bargains for 50 cents to a dollar or two.

Sometimes, you might find a treasure if you're patient and just a bit aggressive. Many auction houses hold weekly consignment auctions on a particular day of the week. Items in these auctions may be assorted or grouped on a theme, such as American folk art. Start attending these on a regular basis. Get to the know the auctioneer. After you've attended a few of his or her auctions, you can boldly go up after the sale is over—usually the auctioneer will stop at a certain time and hold over any items not sold until the following week—and ask if you can buy one of the items that you had your eye on. More often than not, the auctioneer will say yes to your offer and you may walk away with a real find to turn around and sell in your shop.

Individual Sellers

Once your shop is open, people will come to you almost daily with antiques they want to sell. Until then, however, while you're trying to build up stock, you might run an ad in the classified section of your local newspaper, actively soliciting sellers. You can continue this practice after you open the shop if you find it pays off. Such an ad could read like this:

BUYING ANTIQUES
I buy all kinds of antiques.
Must be in good condition.
Call 555–8397

The only real problem you'll run into with buying from individuals is that most of them seem to think they should get, from you, just about the retail value of antiques. They don't understand the realities of markup.

At times someone will respond to your ad and say, "I'm moving and getting rid of everything, including some antiques. Take all or nothing." That's when you go to the seller's house to assess the value of the antiques in the lot. If you feel they're really salable in your shop, you make an offer for everything, based on what you think you can get for the *antiques.* Don't factor into your offering price anything for the rest of the lot.

You haul everything away, place the antiques in your shop, and store the rest. All right, you're thinking, what do I do with all that other stuff—the pots and pans, sheets and towels, romance novels, Tupperware, and ancient typewriters? One option is to hold your own yard sale once a year and get rid of it then. Many dealers do just that and make several hundred dollars or so from all that miscellaneous junk. But you could also give it to the Salvation Army and get a tax credit. The Salvation Army uses any clothing and household goods to help people in need, then sells the rest at its thrift shops. Everyone benefits that way.

Once your shop is open, you can place an attractive sign near your checkout table that informs customers you buy antiques.

Most dealers also put text such as "I buy antiques—one piece or a houseful" on their business cards, then keep a supply of these cards at their checkout table. They make sure each customer leaves with a card, either in his hand or in the bag containing his purchases. Handing out these cards does pay off. Often people will be planning to hold a yard sale but will not want to sell valuable antiques at it. They'll bring them to you.

Yard Sales

The ubiquitous yard sale is an American institution, and what would a weekend be without them? Dealers find it hard to pass up yard sales.

Most people who cruise the yard sales every weekend are casual shoppers, driving from one to another. The serious dealer (that's you), however, knows that to find the salable antiques and collectibles hidden among the plastic kitchenware and cheap florist vases, you must have a plan. Here are some pointers:

- When you read the yard-sale ads on Thursday and Friday evening, mark those that mention antiques or collectibles. Don't waste your time noting those that don't advertise antiques. After all, you must complete your rounds in time to get back home and open your shop.
- As you read the addresses, map a route starting with the sales closest to your home (or those with the earliest starting times) and move on to more distant ones. The purpose is to get to the good sales before someone else snaps up the antiques.
- Every town is different when it comes to finding antiques at good prices at yard sales. You'll have to make your own judgment in this respect about your town. You'll usually find more antiques at the lowest prices in older, middle-class neighborhoods. In many cases owners of these homes have lived there for years and years and have stored a mass of castoffs in their attics and basements. These people are usually not trying to get top dollar for their things. They just want to get rid of them.
- By contrast, the owners of homes in upper-class neighborhoods are usually quite knowledgeable about antiques values. At their sales they set close to retail prices on

any antique or collectible, so you'll seldom find much to buy at such sales.

- At yard sales possession is nine-tenths of the law, so to speak. The unwritten code of the yard sale is that whoever has his hands on an item first has dibs on it. You need to be able to pick things up quickly and hold on to them. Take along a large sturdy plastic tote bag, into which you can drop anything that interests you. This way, you can pick up and carry much more than you could in your arms alone. Then examine your finds carefully, put anything that isn't promising back on the tables, pay for the antiques you do want, and move quickly to the next sale.

To be honest, you probably won't find an antique or collectible of outstanding value at a yard sale. You'll find china, glassware, pottery, and kitchen collectibles, all of modest value. Every once in a while, you'll come upon a piece of furniture—a bed, small table, brass bridge lamp, framed mirror, or whatever. Inevitably, these finds must be refinished, polished, or rewired to make them salable.

Every dealer has at least one story of a spectacular discovery, a real treasure bought for a pittance. A dealer in Ohio discovered four sterling silver steak knives at a not-too-promising yard sale. On one table sat a worn pink satin jewelry box displaying a medley of cheap jewelry in its upper tray. She was about to move on when her instincts told her to pull out the lower drawer in the case. There, dropped in among more cheap jewelry, lay four antique sterling silver steak knives. Hurriedly, she picked them up and dashed to the seller. "How much for these knives?" she asked. "Oh, four dollars," the seller replied. After she had paid for them, she asked the seller why he sold the knives for four dollars. The seller's reply? "We have a new set of stainless steel and those didn't match." The knives were worth a minimum of $250!

One hint about buying at estate sales, auctions, and yard sales: Take at least one of the current antiques and collectibles price guides with you. Otherwise, unless you have a phenomenal memory, you'll have a hard time remembering the thousands of ever changing retail values of items you'll run across.

Some dealers learn this lesson the hard way. Many novice dealers go to yard sales without taking any price guides along. A dealer might find an item he thinks is priced well, but he doesn't know for sure. If he had brought along a general antiques and collectibles price guide, he'd have been able to decide if the price were too high or if he should make the purchase. If he left the sale to check on the price back home, he might return and find the item had been sold.

Other Dealers

Dealers also buy from one another, receiving the customary dealer's 10 percent discount. Many owners of antiques shops make a regular practice of cruising the shops of other dealers. We're usually looking for antiques that are underpriced. Perhaps the dealer got an exceptionally good deal on the antique and priced it low, hoping for a quick sale, or maybe the dealer simply didn't know the value of the antique.

Sometimes you'll have a customer who wants a specific item and will pay you a premium for locating it. At other times you'll be looking for "orphan" pieces to fill out a set. For whatever reason, you'll be searching for antiques you can buy at prices low enough to sell and still make a profit.

The obvious and natural reaction you'll have when you sell an antique to a dealer is, "I didn't price it high enough!" Don't be upset. You'll make some profit, and the other dealer will make some profit. Next week you may buy an underpriced antique from him!

Buying Trips

Once you're established and have a strong feel for what your customers will buy, you may want to go on extensive annual buying trips. Many longtime dealers do just this, taking off for Iowa or Maine or some other area and buying dozens of small tables, dressers, hall trees, and other pieces of furniture. They fill box upon box with china, silver, glassware, jewelry, prints, and other antiques. Most of these dealers drive large trucks that are capable of holding all their purchases.

This is a fine idea as long as a few things fall into place. You can't be off for several weeks in another part of the country buying antiques and in your shop selling them at the same time. If you don't have a partner to keep the shop open, you'll have to either close the shop or hire someone to keep it open for you. To a large extent your decision would be based on your record of sales. If, for example, after one year in business you find your sales are low during January and February, as they are in many antiques shops, you might plan to close the shop for two or three weeks and do your buying then. If sales are consistent year-round, however, you could hire a salesperson to manage the shop while you're gone.

Buying trips can be difficult if you're on your own. If you aren't accustomed to it, you may not feel comfortable driving large trucks for long distances. Many people don't have the shoulder muscles necessary to lift heavy furniture into these trucks by themselves.

An alternative to this is to drive a van, fill it as you go with small items packed in sturdy boxes, and ship larger pieces home by freight. While shipping adds to the cost of the items, you won't have the expense or hassle of driving a large truck.

Pickers

At one time did you cruise your neighborhood yard sales every weekend, casually buying a small antique or two for your own home? That was fun, wasn't it? Perhaps that's where you caught the antiques bug that finally made you decide to open a shop. The antiques world includes hundreds of men and women who do the same thing, only they buy these antiques not for themselves but for the owners of antiques shops. These people are called "pickers."

Here's how the picker system works. You create a network of pickers from among people who want the fun and potential profit of buying and selling antiques but who don't want the responsibility of managing a shop. You can recruit these people from among your friends, from people who come to your shop offering their services as pickers, or by simply putting the word out to other dealers and antiques collectors that you're in the market for pickers.

You tell these people the types of antiques you want to buy and what you're willing to pay for them. The prices you can pay pickers for the antiques they bring you depend to a large extent on the condition of the antiques, whether you have to repair or refinish them, and their salability. You don't guarantee to buy everything they bring to you. It's up to them to know what you can readily sell in your shop and to buy at prices low enough to make a profit when they subsequently sell the antiques to you.

For example, there might be a good market in your area for small antique pitchers that retail between $15 and $29. If you, as owner of the shop, have to go out and search for these pitchers yourself, you probably would be willing to pay the sellers between $4.00 and $7.00 for them, but the time you'd have to invest in locating these pitchers is worth something.

Taking in Antiques on Consignment

Question: I need more good stock to fill my shop, yet my funds are limited after remodeling. How can I acquire quality antiques without an extra outlay of funds?

Answer: You can do so by taking in antiques on consignment. This can provide you with three important benefits:

1. You don't have to buy the antiques out of your own funds, which may be limited at first.
2. By selecting good-quality consignment items, you increase the look of substance in your shop.
3. When those antiques sell, you receive a nice commission.

Commission rates vary from area to area, shop to shop. A very few dealers charge as little as 20 percent; other set rates as high as 50 percent. The average seems to be about 30 percent. Check around and find out what other dealers in your area are charging, then do the same.

You'll probably want to modify your commission policy a bit on very expensive items. For instance, if you normally charge 30 percent commission on consignment items but someone brings in an expensive item that needs to sell for $5,000 and over, you could lower your commission to 15 percent and still make a tidy sum.

As an example of how consignment selling works, let's call the person owning the antique Mike and the person owning the shop Kitty. Mike has a walnut side table he wants to sell. He goes to Kitty and asks if she'll take it in and sell it in her shop on consignment. She examines the piece, decides it's good quality and should sell, and agrees to place it in her shop. She explains that her commission is 30 percent on consignment sales. When the table sells for $300, she retains $90 as her commission and Mike gets the remaining $210.

One bit of advice about the antiques you take on consignment: Whether they happen to be Oriental vases or mahogany beds, beveled mirrors or sets of china, you'd be wise to take only high-quality items that will sell for above-average prices. The reason is simply economics: Your commission on high-priced antiques is more than on low-priced items.

Let's say you're offered two library tables to sell on consignment. They're about the same size, and both are equally desirable in your area. The first is a turn-of-the-century oak table, which has a selling price of $275. The second table is a fine mahogany piece, which can bring $600. You take in both tables and place them in the shop. Each one takes up approximately 9 square feet of the selling floor. Four months later both tables sell on the same day. Your commission (at 30 percent) on the first table is only $82.50; on the second table, it's $180.00. You're making almost $100 more on the higher-priced table, yet it has required no more display space than the lower-priced one and you probably spent no more time showing and selling it.

If you have plenty of stock yourself, however, you'd be foolish to give up 9 square feet to a consignment antique. Suppose you have a nice library table of the same size as the ones in the above example. You paid $200 for it and price it at $600 (a reasonable markup). When the table sells, your profit is $400, far more than for either of the consignment tables.

Accepting antiques to sell on consignment, therefore, is usually a good policy only if you have plenty of space and not enough of your own antiques to fill that space.

Many dealers seldom take items on consignment unless they know the person who owns them. Why? Because too many people place too high a value on their antiques, especially since *Antiques Roadshow* has aired on PBS television stations. The antiques may also be family pieces and, thus, have sentimental value. Or perhaps the owners bought them in an area with higher prices. Whatever the reason, the owners aren't too logical about setting reasonable selling prices on their antiques. They simply want too much for them, and they expect them to sell quickly, not realizing that a valuable antique can take months to sell. As a result, most dealers do business only with people who understand the realities of selling antiques.

You're probably wondering about the legal ramifications of this system. After all, you're taking someone else's valuable property into your shop. Almost all dealers have some kind of written agreement between them and consignors. It can be as simple as a typed sheet or as formal as one generated on a computer and printed in a print shop.

You can make up your own consignment agreement, but the form on page 118 is typically used by many dealers. You'll notice on this form that you, as owner of the shop, don't accept responsibility for the consignor's antiques. Your own insurance covers your property and stock in the case of fire or theft, but it probably won't cover consignment antiques. Can the consignor be protected? Maybe. Some homeowner's policies will cover loss or damage of a consigned antique. Many won't. This is the reason you have a written agreement—to forestall any unpleasantness with your consignor in case of a problem.

One dealer learned the value of such an agreement too late. He took in a lovely Vaseline bowl on consignment, without any written agreement, and agreed verbally to price it at $75. He placed the bowl on the floor while rearranging some stock on an upper shelf. A heavy bookend fell off the shelf and landed squarely on the Vaseline bowl. Horrified, he watched it shatter into a dozen pieces. Since he didn't have an understanding with the owner of the bowl about loss or damage, he felt morally obligated to reimburse her with $75 out of his shop funds.

So, your pickers know you'll pay them between $5.00 and $8.00 for salable pitchers. They scout secondhand stores, yard sales, consignment auctions, thrift shops, and so forth, looking for pitchers they can pick up for small sums. You pay the pickers $5.00 to $8.00 for the pitchers they bring in, and they make a profit on each one they sell to you. Your profit margin when you sell the pitchers is lower than if you had found the pitchers yourself, but you haven't invested any of your time in locating them.

Some pickers in large cities or in areas where there are many antiques dealers make substantial incomes from their business. Most pickers in less populated areas, however, don't expect to make a living from picking. They just want the fun of searching for the antiques as you did at one time. Those who work diligently, though, and come up with good buys can often create nice little side incomes for themselves. Some pickers even take cellular phones along and call a dealer when they come upon an outstanding but pricey item. This way, they know in advance if the dealer is interested.

Inventory of Another Shop

You can create instant inventory for your shop by simply buying out the stock of a dealer who's going out of business. This isn't at all unusual. It's fine as long as you have the finances for the purchase, but the outlay can be considerable.

Sample Consignment Agreement

Date _____

Received from _____

Address _____

Phone number _____

Description of antique _____

_____

Price to be set on antique _____

Commission rate _____

The antique will remain in the shop and on display until _____ ,
on which date the consignor is responsible for picking it up unless other arrangements
are made between consignor and consignee.

   It is understood that the consignee is not responsible for damage or theft of the
antique while it is in his shop.

Signed,

_____

Consignor

_____

Consignee

First, wipe it with a rag wrung out in warm, soapy water, then rinse. That'll remove most dirt. If a layer of grimy residue remains—perhaps pollution from smoke—dampen a rag with mineral spirits and go over the frame again. That should do it.

More often than not, however, the frames that you find will need some TLC to make them salable. Should you be interested in doing this, you'll find an entire chapter devoted to refinishing frames in *How to Recognize and Refinish Antiques*, also published by The Globe Pequot Press.

Books. Old books are always more valuable if their dust jackets are intact. But dust jackets don't always protect old books from dust.

If you need to clean the books in your shop, use the techniques favored by museums and archivists at large libraries. To remove dust from backs, place a layer of cheesecloth over the brush attachment of your vacuum hose, turn the power to low, and sweep front and back carefully.

The same caveat about old paper exists here as it does with old art on paper. Don't take a chance on damaging book pages if they appear to be fragile. Just leave them alone. Smudges on book pages in good condition, however, will respond to a special pink eraser, sold as Pink Pearl or Opaline, that you can buy at an artist's supply store.

Linens. Many old linens will arrive in your hands embellished with brown stains. Most of these stains won't disappear with regular washing, since they've been there for generations. You can, however, sometimes remove an old stain with a method used by savvy antiques dealers. Dampen the piece, then make a paste of your regular laundry detergent and color-safe bleach. Rub the paste into the stain, apply more paste on top of the stain, then place the fabric in the sun for a few hours. A gentle washing will then often remove all or most of the stain.

Ink spots, if not too old, can usually be removed by applying a dab of toothpaste, rubbing gently, then rinsing.

Scorch marks, if not too dark, will lighten when rubbed with white vinegar.

You can't avoid having to iron most old linens before placing them in your shop, but crocheted doilies are another matter. After you wash old doilies, you can give them a fresh, just-ironed look by dipping them in liquid starch, then spreading them on a terry towel that's laid on a carpet or rug. Stretch the doilies out, then anchor the edges with pins. Once dry, the doilies will be very salable.

China. Old china cups often have an undesirable brown tea-and-coffee stain. Remove this by rubbing with a mixture of salt and vinegar.

Another type of brown stain on china occurs simply from age. You'll see this often on platters, bowls, plates, and so forth. One of the best and safest ways to remove this stain is with household bleach. Fill or immerse the piece in bleach and let it soak for a few hours. In most cases the stain will disappear.

Tiny brown hairline cracks often respond to bleach too. Soak the piece in bleach, or if that isn't practical because of the piece's size, dab bleach on the line with cotton swabs. Repeat the dabbing every few hours until the line lightens.

An alternative method is to dissolve two or three denture cleaner tablets in a dishpan filled halfway with hot water. Immerse the stained china, especially stoneware pieces, into the solution and let them soak for twenty-four hours.

Candleholders. Glass, silver, brass, or china candleholders can be cleaned and polished with any of the above methods. You must remove any residual wax first, though. The easiest way is to soak the piece in warm water until the wax softens. You can pick out most of it, then wipe off any remaining wax with a paper towel. Candleholders that can't be dunked in water, such as wooden ones, require different treatment. Just put them in your refrigerator until the wax becomes brittle. You can then carefully chip it off with a blunt knife.

Leather. The best cleaner for leather is usually not saddle soap but a mild solution of warm water and a gentle, nonacid-based, clear facial-quality soap (Neutrogena). Most genuine leather has a faint grain, which was the direction in which the hair grew on the hide. Always wipe along the grain if you can find one.

Try not to spot-clean leather. The best results occur when you work on entire sections. Clean quickly, trying not to soak the leather; wipe with clear water; and dry with a soft cloth.

Marble. Even though marble appears to be rock-hard, it actually has enough porosity to absorb dirt. You can clean mildly dirty marble by scrubbing with a regular household cleaning brush and dishwashing detergent.

If the marble is really grimy, you'll have to get a bit sterner with it. Make a paste of household bleach or hydrogen peroxide and flour to the consistency of heavy cream. Wet the marble with either bleach or peroxide and spread a thick layer of the paste over the entire piece. Cover the marble with plastic wrap and seal the edges tightly. This will keep the paste from drying out.

Place the marble in a cool area, out of the sun. Allow the paste to work for several days, then rinse it off.

You'll often find more stubborn stains on antique marble that tops old dressers, commodes, and small tables. Organic stains (tea, coffee, tobacco, ink, and the like) that didn't succumb to the first bleach/peroxide-flour treatment will usually respond to an additional remedy. Buy whiting from the hardware store and mix it and hydrogen peroxide together into a thick paste, add a few drops of household ammonia, and layer onto the stain. Place a bowl over this mixture to retain moisture and let it sit for a couple of days, then rinse.

This method has little effect on rust stains from metal. To eliminate them, you'll have to use one of the rust removers sold at hardware stores.

Once the marble is free of dirt and stains, polish it with a heavy-duty floor wax.

Note: You can even sand away rough edges on marble. If the marble is in good condition except for generations of dirt and some small chips around the edge, use fine-grain sandpaper and plenty of elbow grease to smooth off the irregularities, then clean it.

White rings on wood. As a rule, these rings, caused by moisture, are easy to remove. Try any one of these remedies:

• Dip a rag in light oil or softened petroleum jelly and rub the ring lightly.
• Dip a piece of fine steel wool in denatured alcohol and rub very gently.
• Dip a rag, dampened in light oil, into cigar or cigarette ash and rub the ring gently.

Decals. Some fifty or sixty years ago, mothers lovingly embellished virtually every high chair and crib with decals of cute little ducks and rabbits. You can remove these decals by soaking them in white vinegar, then scraping gently with a dull table knife.

Christmas ornaments. Antique Christmas ornaments are fast sellers, bringing in high prices, but they're one item you should never make any attempt to clean. The finish on these ornaments is extremely delicate and can rub off at the slightest touch.

Stuffed animals. Cornstarch is the best medium for cleaning old stuffed animals whose pile is dirty. Rub it gently into the pile with your fingers, then let it rest overnight. Next day shake the animal gently, then carefully brush out any remaining cornstarch with a soft brush.

course, but not many of them will be looking for high-ticket antiques. You can help bridge those slow months, however, by stocking and displaying a large supply of low- to medium-priced antiques and collectibles. A sterling silver coffeepot may sit on the shelf gathering dust during those months, while you sell many souvenir spoons, prints, linens, and kitchen collectibles.

Taking Advantage of the Tourist Season

On the other side of the seasonal coin, do you have a steady tourist clientele during a particular time of year? Those visitors can be excellent customers, since they're in a spending mood, so cater to their needs and wants. I've found that many tourists will buy small or flat antiques without a qualm, because these things fit easily into a suitcase or carry-on bag. On the other hand, they hesitate to buy a large or bulky antique even if they genuinely want it. In most cases they'd have to ship the antique home, adding substantially to its cost or the chance of damage.

With this in mind, a couple of weeks before your tourist season starts, you might remove many of your bulkier antiques from the shelves and replace them with those small and flat pieces. Some suggestions: miniature lamps (always a good seller), small dolls, collectible bottles, jewelry, framed needlework, paper goods—sheet music, prints, postcards, fruit labels, photographs, and the like—linens, salt and peppers, sterling silver souvenir spoons, and so forth. Any antique engraved or marked with the name of your town or state is also good.

Nonantiques Inventory

Many dealers add substantially to their profits by carrying a few nonantiques lines. Following are some of the best sellers.

Reference Books

Collectors are always looking for books to help them learn more about their hobbies or to help them identify pieces they own. These books are easy sales in your shop.

Hundreds of such books have been written by experts on every subject under the sun: dolls, toys, chalkware carnival prizes, marbles, majolica, gambling devices, Oriental pottery, Victorian jewelry—you name it, it's in print. I never cease to be amazed at the variety of topics covered in these books. Each book is a valuable source of information for beginning or experienced collectors.

Several distributors wholesale these books to antiques shops, and they all have catalogs from which you'll order. (You'll find some of these distributors listed in the Appendix.) In most cases you have to stock only one book of each title you select, and you buy at a discount of usually 40 percent off the cover price, which allows you to make a decent profit when you sell the books to your customers at the cover prices.

Here's one problem you're almost sure to run up against in carrying reference books. Many of them are fairly expensive, so some of your customers will ask if they can simply browse through a book, looking for a bit of information they need. Be polite, but refuse the request. If you allow this practice, the books will become dirty and dog-eared, and you'll never sell them.

The best solution is to keep the books in a closed glass case where the dustcovers and titles are clearly visible but where customers can't get to them without your permission. You can put a small notice on the shelf, informing your customers that the books are for purchase only and not for browsing.

Plate and Cup-and-Saucer Holders

These inexpensive items, usually retailing for under $2.00, are fast sellers. Keep a few holders on display, and always ask the customer who has just purchased a fine plate or cup and saucer if he needs a holder. Sometimes people buy as many as five or six at a time. Easy profit for you!

Furniture Polish

Many antiques shops carry quality furniture polishes and silver creams as a sideline. These polishes and creams are not ordinary grocery-store brands but the ones used most often by professionals in this business.

After purchasing an antique, a customer will often ask, "What do you recommend I use to clean and care for this walnut commode [or silver vase, or whatever]?" Bring out a bottle or jar of one of your special cleaning or polishing products, and he's almost bound to buy it. The customer will thank you for helping to keep the antique beautiful, and you'll make a few dollars profit. Many manufacturers of these creams and polishes advertise their products in the antiques trade journals.

Handcrafted Accessories

You can add color to your shop *and* your profits by carrying, on consignment, a few handcrafted, old-fashioned-looking decorative accessories. These can be embroidered linens, rag dolls, quilted pillows, pot holders, and so forth. I know of one dealer who always stocks some charming Christmas stockings around the middle of November. The woman who makes the stockings for him fashions them to look as though they are made from old crazy quilts, and she can't keep up with the orders. His customers love them!

Just be careful to accept only top-quality crafts, the type you see in the best shops, and beware of loading your shop down with too many artsy-craftsy items. You're really in business to sell antiques, not pillows and pot holders. A few pieces will go a long way toward adding color and charm to your shop, but too many detract from your regular merchandise.

Potpourri

Few things are as nostalgic as fragrant potpourri, and the ambience is perfect for an antiques shop. Place a bowl filled with little bags of potpourri at your checkout table, priced at $3.00 or $4.00 a bag. The bags sell quickly, and they add a pleasant aroma to your shop. Potpourri is a breeze to package too. Just place about one-half cup of prepared potpourri on squares of colorful net, gather the net up, tie with a pretty ribbon, and you're in business. You'll find directions for making potpourri and some recipes on the following pages.

Traditionally, potpourri is made from summer garden flowers, dried, then mixed with spices and aromatic oils. You say you'd like to make some potpourri but don't have a flourishing garden of roses and lavender? Not to worry! There's an easy way to get literally armfuls of colorful roses and other flowers at absolutely no cost. The secret is to make friends

How to Make Fragrant Potpourri

Potpourri is a mixture of five basic ingredients: dried flower petals or other natural material, herbs, spices, essential oils, and fixatives. The resulting fragrance, whether spicy or delicate, woodsy or tangy, depends on the dried materials used and the aroma of the oils blended into the natural materials. Roses, lavender, and tuberoses are the only flowers that retain their natural scent when dried. Other flowers are used to add bulk to the mixture, and the oils to provide the fragrance.

The best potpourris are enjoyed for their color almost as much as for their scent. The drying process nearly always softens the natural color of flower petals (strawflowers are a major exception), so choose the brightest flowers for your own mixtures. Other than strawflowers, some of the best for color are roses, hollyhocks, larkspur, cornflowers, marigolds, heather, purple violets, lilacs, blue delphiniums, and lavender.

Basic Potpourri Mixture

4 quarts dried flower petals

4 tablespoons dried herbs

4 tablespoons crushed spices

2 teaspoons essential oil

4 tablespoons fixative (orrisroot or ground coriander)

(The ingredients listed above are only approximate and may be varied according to what you have available; however, do follow the mixing and storage directions as given.)

This recipe can be adapted to almost any combination of flowers, herbs, and oils:

Mix dried flowers and herbs gently in a large plastic bag. Add crushed spices and mix gently. Sprinkle essential oil over mixture and blend gently with dry ingredients. Sprinkle fixative over mixture and toss lightly to blend. Place potpourri in crock or plastic bag and seal tightly. Mix gently from top to bottom and side to side every three or four days to help the fragrance develop and blend. The potpourri will be mature and ready to use in about one month.

Here are some sample mixtures:

Summer Rose Potpourri

4 quarts dried rose petals and other flowers

4 tablespoons rosemary

2 tablespoons crushed cloves

2 tablespoons crushed cinnamon bark

2 teaspoons essential oil of rose

2 tablespoons orrisroot

2 tablespoons coriander

Happy Holidays Potpourri

4 quarts dried pine needles, finely chipped pine bark,
   and dried berries

2 tablespoons dried mint or eucalyptus leaves

2 tablespoons crushed bay leaves

2 tablespoons marjoram

2 tablespoons crushed nutmeg

2 teaspoons essential oil of pine or sandalwood

4 tablespoons orrisroot

Lavender Lace Potpourri

4 quarts dried lavender and other flower petals

2 tablespoons thyme

2 tablespoons dried mint

4 tablespoons dried orange peel

2 teaspoons oil of lavender

4 tablespoons orrisroot

with your local florists and morticians. These people discard thousands of flowers every year, and most of them are more than happy to let you cart the surplus away.

Florists, for example, have to stock large quantities of flowers for Mother's Day, Valentine's Day, prom nights, Christmas, and so forth. Often on the day following the holiday, they'll have buckets of flowers left over that are a trifle past their prime and can't be sold. These blossoms are perfect for potpourri, though. All you have to do is make arrangements in advance to pick up these leftovers.

Flower arrangements fill a mortuary during a funeral or memorial service, and, in many cases, the family doesn't want to take the flowers home. Ask the mortician to call you whenever a funeral is scheduled. If the flowers are to be discarded, not donated to a hospital or nursing home, all you have to do is go there and load them into your car or truck.

Making and packaging potpourri can be a fine activity to keep you busy in the shop during slow periods.

Gift Certificates

Gift certificates made out on little pieces of paper can provide you with a welcome source of income. So often your customers will come into the shop, browse around, and then say in desperation, "I want to get a gift for my _____ [fill in the blank—son's teacher/mother-in-law/boss/secret pal/next-door neighbor, or whatever], and I have no idea what she would like!" That's when you suggest a gift certificate. The look of relief on your customer's face will make your day, as well as guarantee a sale later on. Some office supply shops carry generic gift certificates, or you can have custom ones printed at a good copy center.

An attractive sign that says GIFT CERTIFICATES AVAILABLE near your checkout table will solve many of your customers' problems, and it'll be like putting money in your bank for you.

Making Sure an Item Is an Antique

To anyone who browses antiques shops these days, the question "What is an antique?" seems to have many answers. Side by side with ancient-looking furniture and old-fashioned

Question: Should I carry reproductions in my shop? If so, what's the accepted way to identify them?

Answer: Some antiques shops do carry a few reproductions, although many dealers frown on the practice, saying it diminishes the value of genuine antiques. You should probably follow the lead of other shops in your area.

Limit reproductions to small items such as black iron match holders, rhinestone jewelry, and the giftware being reissued today by manufacturers, such as Fenton for example, that distributed the same patterns years ago. Just be sure to label each piece "Reproduction" on the price tag.

china, browsers may find ruffled pink glass and souvenir spoons, no older than themselves. The problem bewilders not only buyers but dealers too.

In 1930 the U.S. government ruled that objects had to be *at least one hundred years old* to be classified as antiques and be admitted duty-free into the United States. But that was a legislative tax decision. Since then, antiques have often been defined as objects made before 1830.

In Europe items as recent as that seem quite young. In contrast with a classic Roman head, an eighteenth-century chair is modern. Antiques shops in European cities are often called "antiquities" shops. Except for Native American relics and a few Spanish buildings in the Southwest, the oldest American antiques are about 350 years old.

Yet American dealers experience the same contrast in their shops. To a New England dealer who might sell pine furniture from Pilgrim times, a Victorian sofa doesn't seem antique. But in Iowa or Washington it does, because it represents the earliest furnishings in the region. The age of antiques seems to vary in relation to their environment. And so the perception of "What is an antique?" changes from region to region.

Americans often count among their antiques items made by machine as well as those wrought by hand. Most handmade items date prior to 1830, which serves as the dividing line between the handcrafted age and the machine age.

The salability of an antique can also depend on the story behind it. As a piece gets handed down from generation to generation, its history takes on added flourishes. A spinning wheel made in 1820 becomes the spinning wheel brought over on the *Mayflower*. A bed from 1790 becomes a bed George Washington slept in.

Determining the Age of Furniture

Question: Are there any guidelines I can use to determine the age of a piece of furniture?

Answer: Yes. All old wood furniture can be identified with simple examinations.

- Size and shape of dovetails on drawers. Dovetails on old furniture are always larger and less symmetrical than those on modern pieces.
- Wood grain. Furniture makers about one hundred years ago often constructed tables, dressers, and such, of quartersawn wood. This wood was cut to produce a distinctive wavy pattern, sometimes called tiger oak. This cutting method was extremely wasteful and isn't used today.
- Saw marks. Before the advent of modern machinery, all wood was cut by hand. Whereas cabinetmakers would take great pains to sand and smooth the exterior surface of a piece of furniture, they often left concealed areas quite rough. You can frequently see obvious saw marks on the underside of tables and the backs of case pieces.
- Shrinkage. All wood shrinks in time. With enough time, shrinkage becomes obvious. You'll sometimes see enclosed panels that have split because the cabinetmaker glued the panels into the surrounding framework. The thin panels eventually shrank and the tension caused them to split. Round tables made of a softwood such as pine can become slightly oval in time as the wood shrinks across the grain.
- Normal wear. Any piece of furniture that's been in use for three or four generations is bound to show some wear. The back legs of chairs may be worn where people have leaned back on them. Many case pieces made of softwood will have definite gouges around knobs and handles caused by fingernails hitting the wood. Kneehole desks and dressing tables nearly always have worn areas around their inner edges from chairs being pushed in and out.

Question: What about silver, china, and glassware? They seem much harder to classify as to age.

Answer: Yes, the age of silver, china, and glassware is more difficult to identify, especially since many reproductions are beginning to flood the market. Here, however, are some guidelines:

Because silver is a soft metal, the patterns on antique silverware are often slightly blurred from use and polishing. Old silver also has a soft glow, a patina, rather than the brilliant, hard finish of newly made silver.

A great deal of old pattern glass is being reproduced today, and sometimes it's very difficult to tell the old from the new. However, when a present-day manufacturer produces glassware from old molds, sections of the design will be missing or quite faint. Also, as a rule, the quality of old glass is superior to that of new glass. If in doubt, hold the glass lightly in one hand and tap it with a pencil. Listen for a clear bell-like ring, which indicates that the piece is lead glass. Newer lime glass will thud instead of ring.

New, finely cut crystal, however, is almost indistinguishable from antique crystal. The only clue might be a slight etching of the lower surface from repeated scraping across tables and shelves.

As with crystal, fine old china that's been cared for is extremely difficult to distinguish from modern pieces of the same quality. Again, you'll sometimes find a slight roughness on the lower surfaces, which indicates where the piece has been moved back and forth across tables and shelves. Hold a plate at right angles to a strong light, too, and you might see faint lines in the finish caused by the hundreds of times hungry diners cut their meat there. A sure sign of age, though, is the brown tint and crazing that occurs on much old china and pottery, the result of repeated warming in brick ovens or wood stoves.

But while the personal associations of an heirloom add to its interest, they can't be relied upon to place its date and source. Not all old pieces have a pedigree or a maker's mark or label, but each has characteristics that identify it and make it valuable to someone else. The secret of where and when and by whom it was made is in its material, its design, and its workmanship. So an antique is what dealers and collectors perceive it to be.

If you stock what people in your area want to buy, whether it's a genuine Chippendale or Fiesta ware, you'll make money.

How can you be sure the pieces you buy to resell are genuine antiques and not fakes or reproductions? First, there's a world of difference between *fake antique furniture* and *repro-*

duction furniture. You'll hardly ever be offered fake antique furniture. A fake is a deliberate attempt to deceive by using old construction techniques on wood that's been deliberately distressed to simulate age. The piece is then passed off as an antique. Yes, this does happen, but because the process is so time-consuming, it's usually practiced only by charlatans trying to emulate extremely valuable furniture.

Keep a small, battery-operated black light in your car when you go shopping for stock. It'll help you detect any hidden crack or repair in china. A black light will also illuminate genuine Vaseline glass with that traditional fluorescent glow, helping you differentiate it from ordinary glass.

You'll occasionally read about a table or cabinet, supposedly a fine seventeenth-century French piece perhaps, that sold for many thousands of dollars in some prestigious antiques auction house. It later turns out to be a fake. The chances of any of us being offered such a piece are about as good as winning one of those megamillion-dollar sweepstakes prizes.

Reproduction furniture, on the other hand, is furniture constructed with modern methods in the styles of earlier eras. Some of this furniture is of excellent quality, but no manufacturer ever advertises or sells it as antique. A good example is Shaker chairs. Craftsmen construct reproductions of these finely made pieces using original methods, so most sell for almost as much or the same as the genuine article.

The problem occurs when a reproduction passes from hand to hand, garnering wear along the way until it really looks old. All knowledge of its origin is eventually lost, and the present owner might honestly believe it to be an antique. A well-worn reproduction can fool anyone who doesn't have some information on how furniture looked and was made generations ago.

For more complete information on determining age in furniture, consult *How to Recognize and Refinish Antiques,* another Globe Pequot Press publication.

Chapter Six

Buying and Selling Antiques on the Internet

The Internet is here to stay and it's maturing fast. Most dealers have racked up Internet sales well exceeding their projections. And you can too.

The condition of the antiques market has changed radically since eBay opened for business in late 1995. Until then, collectors built their collections over time. In fact, creating a sizable collection required hours visiting yard and garage sales, flea markets, antiques malls, antiques shows, and auctions. Most collectors frequented shops and malls close to home because they didn't have the means to travel all over the country searching for pieces to add to their collections.

Today, the Internet offers a vast national and international market—eBay, alone, offers over 200,000 antiques and collectibles—that collectors can access from their home computer. Thanks to eBay and online antiques malls, buying and selling antiques online offers a world of possibilities. Ebay, created to sell Pez dispensers, controlled the online antiques market for a while, but the concept caught on and now there are hundreds of Internet auction sites.

The popularity and success of online auctions create opportunities for you. You can use software tools to create eye-catching advertisements, have counters to keep track of how many visitors look at your page or site, and search for the best deals among several sites if you're buying.

This chapter will cover some of the ins and outs of buying and selling antiques through the Internet. You'll find some ideas here that will generate more income for *you* too.

Those of you who are already on the Internet can skip the following section. Just go on to the section headed *Advantages of Buying and Selling on the Internet* on page 139.

How Do I Get on the Internet?

While most home-based antiques dealers connect to the Internet through a dial-up modem using their home telephone line, you can also access it over cable TV or high-speed DSL connections. But to buy and sell online, a dial-up connection will work just fine. Of course, you'll need to know how to use your computer.

Before you begin to use the Internet, you'll need to sign up with an Internet Service Provider (ISP). While there are many choices out there, you need to select one that will be operating almost all the time. Many people sign up with America Online (AOL), but because there are so many people using it, getting online can be a problem at times. It will be in your best interest to sign up with a larger national company like Earthlink, Verizon, or AT&T, rather than a smaller local company because the larger nationals have more resources so there's no waiting or redialing to get online. Monthly rates average about $20 for unlimited service. You can, however, pay less for 150 to 250 hours per month. After your first month online, check to see how many hours you used. If it's under the limited amount, then switch to the lower-rated limited-hour service.

Also, be sure your ISP offers local dial-up numbers. Check with the company about this *before* you sign up. You may find yourself paying hefty long-distance charges over and above your monthly Internet charge.

You'll also need software called a browser that opens to the Internet. Microsoft's Internet Explorer, which comes included with any version of Windows, and Netscape Navigator are the two most commonly used. Once you open your browser window, you can point the browser where you want to go by typing the Internet address or URL (uniform resource locator) into the browser's address line. Every site on the World Wide Web, as the Internet is also called, has its own unique URL.

Web designers use HTML (hypertext markup language) to create Web pages and sites. These hypertext links allow you to go from one site to another or one page to another or one part of a page to another. Every Web site also has a domain name preceded by www, which stands for World Wide Web. Most of the domain names of the antiques sites you'll be visiting are followed by .com, which stands for "commercial."

But the Internet is huge—several billion sites strong. So you'll need to use what's called a search engine to find what you're looking for. One of the best search engines is Google (www.google.com). By typing a keyword—that is, a word or phrase that directly represents what you're looking for, such as "Parian Ware"—into the Google keyword space, then clicking on "Google Search," you'll be given a list of sites that result from your search. You can search either for Web sites themselves or the images on them.

Advantages of Buying and Selling on the Internet

- *Eliminates time-consuming shopping for stock.* Locating salable stock can take lots of time. You can spend hours each week attending auctions, estate sales, responding to "for sale" ads in the newspaper. Sometimes you come back with a car full of quality stock, sometimes it's time totally wasted. But shopping for stock online is *fast.* All it takes is just a few clicks of the mouse.

  A big problem faced by most dealers who manage their shops alone is even being able to scout out the estate/garage sales and auctions. The best buys at estate and garage sales are always on Fridays. Auctions are nearly always held on Saturdays. Yet weekends are the times an antiques shop should be open and the owner there to attend to customers. If a dealer doesn't have a savvy friend, willing spouse, or excellent part-time help, she simply can't attend those weekend sales.

  Online selling, though, goes on twenty-four hours a day, seven days a week. A dealer can buy when it's convenient for her.

- *Is ideal for dealers in out-of-the-way locations.* Many small towns offer few consistently reliable places to buy a wide variety of stock. However, every day the Internet lists thousands of antiques for sale—all prices, all periods, all descriptions. At online auctions, you can find everything from an Elvis record going for $5.00 to an emerald and diamond necklace listed for over $5,000.00.

  So any dealer who buys on the Internet can stock a wide selection of salable inventory—funky fifties memorabilia, trendy Art Deco accessories, and genuine quality antiques. Customers will return again and again because they know they'll always find new and interesting items to purchase. This isn't the case in shops managed by dealers who rely only on local or area sources for their stock. Too often the choice in one shop is almost identical to that in another shop.

- *Assists part-time antiques dealers.* For various reasons, some home-based dealers do not maintain their shops on a full-time basis. A few may be keeping their other jobs until they build up a reliable antiques clientele, and so open their home-based shops only during certain hours or on weekends. Those dealers can buy and sell on the Internet whenever they have a free hour or two.

More often, though, part-time dealers are those who live in areas where they make a substantial part of their income from the tourist trade. They'll stay open long hours seven days a week during the summer, but close up for two or three months midwinter. Harsh weather in some parts of the country can virtually eliminate the tourist trade.

During those same months few locals will brave a raging blizzard to shop for antiques. But the dealers can sit home on cold, snowy days, relax by the fire, and through the Internet buy enough stock to carry them for months once they open in the spring.

- *Eases shopping for special orders.* Few things can do more to inspire enthusiasm among an antiques dealer's customers than for her to be able to fill special orders. Yet, this can be a genuine problem if the dealer has to rely on traditional buying sources.

How often, for example, can the average dealer locate a cup and saucer of an obscure pattern to fill out a customer's china set? Yet, if that dealer closely watches items listed on the Internet, the chances are good someone out there has just that cup and saucer for sale. One more sale made. One more happy customer.

- *Reaches customers worldwide.* No longer do antiques dealers have to depend upon customers in their own locality. By using the Internet a dealer in New Orleans or Seattle or Newark or anywhere in between can sell to customers in Tokyo, London, Toronto, or virtually any other city in the free world.

- *Sells unique items.* You may someday come upon an especially unique antique or collectible, one perhaps desired by only half a dozen people on the planet. Most dealers who maintain shops would pass that item up, knowing the chances of one of those six people coming into the shop are virtually impossible.

Yet, the very collectors of those unique items scan the Internet regularly, searching for one more piece to fill out their collections.

A dealer at an estate sale discovered, along with a few other items, two strange brass tubes that contained an apparatus he didn't understand. His instinct kicked in, though, and he paid $5.00 for the two. He did some research and discovered the tubes were two of the earliest calculators, invented in Germany sixty years ago—a rare find indeed.

The dealer immediately listed them on eBay. Within the week he sold each tube for a hundred times that $5.00 to a fellow in Tokyo who collects just such devices.

- *Develops regular customers for certain collectibles.* Certainly, every home-based antiques dealer tries to cultivate regular customers by searching for items that will fill out their collections. Dealers on the Internet do the same. The difference is that the Internet dealer has a vastly larger audience than the dealer who only maintains a shop.

One dealer specializes in selling collectible books and cameras. Now that he's expanded to selling on the Internet he has more than doubled his clientele list. He has a loyal following of buyers there who look for his dealer number among the dozens of dealers selling on the Internet. They know the items he lists will be of top quality and well worth the asked price.

Disadvantages of Buying and Selling on the Internet

- *Prices are not wholesale.* Yes, as terrific as it may sound, there *are* downsides to buying and selling on the Internet, especially for the dealer who decides to make it her primary selling mode. This is a growing trend, so you should know the hazards.

Remember that many, if not most, of the buyers on the Internet are *collectors*, not dealers who plan to sell everything they buy there. Collectors are usually willing to pay a reasonable retail price for any item that will help fill out their collections.

With that in mind, the final bid for any desirable antique or collectible is almost bound to reach that reasonable retail price. Often it will go much higher, just as happens at a traditional auction.

Dealers can hardly pay that high price and still expect to resell the item for a profit. The profit has already been made by the seller of the item, who purchased it at a much lower price somewhere else, then offered it for sale on the Internet, figuring to make her usual profit when it sold. A subsequent dealer/buyer would have to factor in *her* own overhead to the purchase price, plus add a percentage for profit. (See Chapter 7 for a discussion on markup as it relates to profit.) The resulting figure (auction purchase price + overhead + profit) she'd have to list as a *minimum* starting bid for the item would be more than most collectors would pay.

For that reason, many dealers don't buy on the Internet.

• *There's no place for socializing.* Another, more personal, disadvantage of buying and selling on the Internet is the lack of one-on-one contact with customers. One of the reasons most people enjoy dealing in antiques is the personal contact they have with their customers. Lovers of antiques get just as much pleasure talking about their collections as they do bragging about their children or relating the latest antic their cat pulled.

There's little of that on the Internet. Regular dealers on the Internet do develop a few customers who contact them personally by e-mail, but the number is negligible.

In most cases the relationship between sellers and buyers is purely business— an item is offered, some faceless buyer makes a high bid. Money arrives in the mail. The seller ships the antique. The seller and buyer know no more about one another after the transaction than they did before.

You may feel as if you're on a production line. You're a conveyer belt taking in antiques and dispersing them with no more intimate association than if they were automobile tires or pot scrubbers.

The issue of fraud on the Internet is discussed on page 145.

Selling through Internet Auction Sites

Several sites on the Internet now hold either auctions or outright sales of antiques for dealers. You'll need to register with them before you can buy or sell, but there's no fee for registration. The process is quite simple and easily handled with simple directions online.

Yahoo (www.yahoo.com) offers a cornucopia of information for anyone interested in selling or buying antiques on the Internet. Click onto its link "auctions" and then "help" and you'll find answers to many of your questions. For example, you'll find paragraphs describing how to upload photographs to illustrate your antiques, write descriptions that will interest buyers, and when to set reserve prices. By searching through various links you can amass a great deal of valuable information that will help you list, price, and sell your antiques and collectibles.

At this writing, eBay and Yahoo control two of the largest antiques auction sites, eBay being the larger, with tens of millions of registered customers. The online auctions are almost identical, and Yahoo seems to offer sellers the same volume of buyers as eBay.

To register with eBay go to the Web site at www.ebay.com and click on the "sign in" link. You'll be asked to "click here to register." After you answer a couple of questions the registration form will come up on the screen. You'll fill in your name, address, phone number, and e-mail address. You'll be given an identification number, after which you'll be registered to buy and sell on eBay.

Registering to buy and sell on Yahoo is quite similar. You can go directly to the auctions section of Yahoo at auctions.yahoo.com. Find the link marked "account info.," follow the on-screen directions, and you'll soon be registered with Yahoo.

After registering with Yahoo or eBay, dealers may list one item or a dozen on these sites, but the most successful dealers have dozens of antiques and collectibles for sale at any one time. You may be a dealer on both sites if you like, but you should not list the same item on each at the same time. That's a no-no in this business.

To list an item you'll fill out a short on-screen form that asks you to describe the item, tell which category it should be in, state the minimum bid you'll accept, and determine how long you wish it to be listed.

Since eBay and Yahoo contain thousands of listings on any given day, most serious buyers click directly onto the specific categories that interest them. One buyer may only want to bid on Civil War memorabilia, so he'll go directly to that site. Another may be trying to fill out a set of Haviland china, so she goes to that site, ignoring all others. For those reasons, you should be quite specific when listing the category of any antique or collectible.

It's almost mandatory to include a clear photograph along with your antique's description. Ebay offers instructions on how to do this. You can use a scanner or a digital camera to transfer an image to the screen. With the cost of a good 2.0- to 3.0-megapixel digital camera, which is sufficient for taking photos to be used online, at $200 to $300, many antiques dealers are opting to take their own photos.

Since this is an auction, not a retail shop, is there any way to determine what the eventual high bid on an antique might be? Sometimes. You can set what's called a "reserve" when you list the antique. This reserve is the minimum price you would accept as a final bid. If that minimum is not met, the antique is pulled from the auction. However, the auction sites will probably list the antique again at no cost to you.

Instead of setting a reserve figure, some dealers simply list the antique with no minimum bid. They take their chances that the final bid will be high enough for them to make a profit on the antique. That can be risky. I would suggest you study the auction sites carefully and watch for final bids on antiques. In your opinion, are purchase prices in line with the value of antiques? Could you have made a profit on similar items selling them at those figures?

Most dealers list a closing date for bidding on any item. The average seems to be about one week from the time the antique comes up for auction. The bidding for that item will end on that date and the person entering the highest bid at that time will be awarded the antique. Bidding sometimes becomes hot and heavy when the clock is running out on a desirable antique.

Once a high bid is received and accepted, the auction site puts the seller and buyer in contact with one another. It's up to them, then, to work out the payment and delivery arrangements. They usually communicate with one another through e-mail.

Most antiques dealers who sell online accept either money orders, cashier's checks, or personal checks as payment for an antique. A few accept Mastercard and Visa. In the case of personal checks, the dealer waits until they clear before shipping the item.

Buyers over the Internet can be incredibly trusting of the dealers. One dealer told me he sold a rare manuscript for $455. The buyer said payment would be coming immediately.

It arrived within three days—cash! He had stuffed the bills into a plain envelope that didn't even have a security lining.

Dealers always add shipping costs to the purchase price of anything bought over the Internet.

How Reliable Are Internet Purchases?

When I heard about *buying* antiques on the Internet, my first reaction was "How can anyone be sure the purchased item is as described? Suppose it's damaged? Cracked? Chipped? Torn? Even worse—a reproduction!" How can a seller be sure she will be paid for the antique?"

Dealers who sell on the Internet are rated, both by the site (eBay, Yahoo, or whatever) and by the buyers. Each dealer's identifying number accompanies every offer to sell.

The auction sites encourage buyers to report their experiences in dealing with individual dealers. Does that dealer ship promptly? Is the merchandise well packed? Is the antique exactly as described and as pictured? One or two poor ratings might simply be sour grapes, but more than that usually means the dealer is not legitimate. If complaints continue she could well be dropped by the site as a dealer.

Buyers are also rated—by dealers. Each buyer has an identifying number as well and that number comes up on the screen whenever the buyer makes a high bid for an item. If for any reason the purchase doesn't go through, the dealer makes a complaint to the site. Maybe the buyer's check wasn't good. Maybe she backed out after the bidding closed and reneged on the purchase. Dealers know then to avoid taking bids from that person.

Regular professional buyers and sellers understand this rating system. It helps them make businesslike decisions about their transactions. You'll quickly catch onto the system, too, once you start buying and selling on the Internet.

The vast majority of sales on the Internet go through with no problems. Getting paid for an antique you sell is seldom a problem. Ask for a money order, a credit card number, or a cashier's check as payment before you ship the item. If the winning bidder backs out and doesn't send payment, you can always contact the person who was the next highest bidder in the auction and see if she wants to buy.

But suppose you have a complaint about something *you* buy. Maybe the item is damaged or not as represented. What do you do? If you feel you've been defrauded, you do have resources. First, contact the Web site itself. You may be asked to try to resolve the problem yourself with the seller. That can be accomplished via e-mail, regular mail, telephone, or fax. One of those methods will nearly always unravel the difficulty, which usually results from a lack of communication or misinformation.

If you're still not satisfied, you can go a step further. The Yahoo auction site suggests several alternatives, including contacting an arbitrator through links to such services on their site. The Better Business Bureau is a source if the seller is a business. Mail fraud issues can be addressed to the United States Postal Service or the U.S. Attorney General.

The eBay auction site has a different set of guidelines for unhappy buyers. It offers sellers and buyers $200 in insurance against proven fraud. The Web site spells out details for obtaining this insurance. Then, as with Yahoo, eBay asks you to contact the seller and try to work out the problem. If this one-on-one mediation fails, you can file a fraud report with the site. Ebay will then contact the seller and try to get a resolution. If all else fails you can then file a claim for insurance.

Now, what is it going to cost you to sell your antiques on the Internet? Registration with the auction sites is free. However, there are selling charges. Both Yahoo and eBay charge a listing fee. This can be as low as 5 cents for an item listed at less than $10.00 to $2.00 for those listed for over $50.00.

Once a sale is consummated, you'll be charged a small commission, based on the selling price. Right now that is on a sliding scale ranging from 2 percent to 5 percent. Once you're registered with an auction site, you'll be given a detailed rundown of these charges.

Selling through Internet Antiques Malls: TIAS

TIAS is an online site that's quite similar to a traditional antiques mall. Instead of placing antiques up for auction with no real guarantee as to the final selling price (as with eBay and Yahoo), TIAS places them in an online catalog from which collectors buy. The dealer sets a firm price on the item and it is listed at that figure. No bidding.

Though small compared to the auction sites, TIAS now offers more than 800 dealers, but it has one advantage for those of us who are antiques dealers: TIAS lists *only* antiques and collectibles, instead of a wide variety of merchandise. And these antiques are listed in traditional antiques categories. So, theoretically at least, it's easier for collectors to locate the items they want.

TIAS dealers are required to maintain a minimum of at least one hundred items for sale at all times, and the combined value must be at least $5,000. Each item must be illustrated with a photograph. Unlike the auction sites, TIAS dealers must maintain some sort of a physical address—either a street address or a post office box number. They must provide a minimum of a seven-day return policy on anything sold through the site.

TIAS offers its dealers a choice of two packages: a 10 percent commission on the antiques sold or a flat fee based on the amount of space used on the site by the dealer. Most dealers choose the first option since they pay nothing if nothing sells.

If you do not already have a merchant credit card account, TIAS will provide one for a one-time fee of $100. For more information about becoming a TIAS dealer, go to the Web site at www.tias.com. Click on the "sell" link. You'll be given complete information about TIAS, then asked for your e-mail address. Within minutes you can be registered and ready to begin listing your antiques for sale.

TIAS dealers may remove an antique from the site at will or keep it listed as long as they like. Is there a disadvantage to this policy? Some dealers think there is. Some sell only through the auctions, not through TIAS. Why? To make a living dealers must have a fast turnover of their merchandise. That turnover averages about six to seven days from the time they list an item on eBay until it sells. Some TIAS dealers keep their merchandise listed on TIAS for much longer before finding a buyer. But many just can't afford that time frame.

Selling through Your Own Web Site

This is an option, of course, and you can certainly look into it.

Some computer manuals give detailed instructions on how to set up your own Web site. You can also buy software that will walk you through the process. You might get the necessary instruction if you live near a college or university that offers adult education courses in computers. Many computer-literate high school or college students would welcome the opportunity to set up your site—for a fee, of course. Or you can hire a technician at your Internet server to design one for you.

After determining that the domain name you choose is available, you'll register it online. You'll pay a fee that will cover the use of that name for a certain period, usually two years. You can then design your own Web site.

Some points to remember:

- Make the design attractive with pleasing graphics, *but* keep it simple and easy to navigate (no irritating flashing lights or loud music).
- Choose a Web site address that will be easy for your clients to remember.

While thousands of companies now have their own Web sites, home-based antiques dealers are more likely to sell through eBay or Yahoo or one of the online antiques malls.

Eliminate the Home Shop Altogether?

Here's an idea for those of you who, for whatever reason, aren't able to or don't want to maintain an antiques business in your home right now. Maybe you will in the future, but the Internet offers you other options.

The Internet can provide you with a way to enter the antiques business while still employed elsewhere.

Some dealers rent space in local antiques malls where someone else takes care of the selling. They search for antiques and collectibles on weekends during their days off, then take them to the malls. While this can work out well and you can make some money, you may discover that you can make more by selling those same items on the Internet.

After successfully selling antiques and collectibles on the Internet, you can establish yourself as a dealer and set up an online shop.

Chapter Seven

Overhead, Pricing, and Markup

Profit may not be your only reason for opening an antiques shop. It isn't for many people. You enjoy working with antiques, and you know you'll grow to love the camaraderie that exists between owners of small shops, their customers, and other dealers. During slow times you can sit and chat with friends about your favorite subject—antiques.

You wouldn't be in the business, however, if you didn't expect a reasonable return on your financial investment. You also expect to be compensated for your time spent in researching current values, studying trends, and locating the antiques you'll sell.

To achieve a good return, you need to know more than antiques themselves. You need to understand how to price your antiques to make a profit. The Small Business Administration suggests you take three main factors into consideration as you price your antiques:

1. your overhead in operating your shop
2. your time and research involved in buying the antiques
3. the demands of the market

The Realities of Overhead

Some first-time dealers in antiques have trouble factoring the operating expenses or the overhead of their shops into the prices they place on their antiques. Too many of them underestimate the amount of money it will take to keep the doors open, and they therefore underprice their antiques. They think that if they buy an antique for $25 and sell it for $50, they've made $25 profit—not by a long shot. Don't fall into this trap. Out of that $25 must come a portion of all your overhead expenses.

Your overhead is those nonmerchandise expenses as listed in the chart on pages 88–89, and will probably include a portion of your rent or mortgage payments, taxes, utilities, and home insurance. You'll also have to include your shop telephone, insurance on your stock, professional services from an attorney and accountant, advertising, employees (if any), professional books and subscriptions, vehicle expenses, supplies, and maintenance on your home/shop.

Some of your expenses—mortgage or rent payments, supplies, and so forth—will remain pretty much the same from month to month. Others, however—taxes and insurance for example—will be paid quarterly, not monthly. Attorney fees may occur only two or three times a year. The cost of utilities varies widely from midwinter to midsummer.

As a result, a record of expenses and income for one month, such as those listed on pages 90–91, is not really indicative of your overall overhead and profit. Although these monthly figures are certainly valuable in helping you know early on whether you're heading in the right direction, they reflect your overhead and income *only for* that one month. To come up with realistic figures on your overall overhead, you must calculate your expenses and income on an *annual* basis. Your cash flow statement is a big help in this respect.

In Chapter 4 you saw how to figure your nonmerchandise expenses per month and how to forward the expenses from one month to the next, resulting in an annual total of expenses. At the end of the year, you'll divide that annual total of expenses by 12 for a rough estimate of your overhead per month. As noted in Chapter 3, you'll probably want to adjust many aspects of your business plan at the end of your first year in business. This figure—average overhead per month—will be one of those adjustments. To make a profit, you have to price your antiques to cover their initial costs, plus your average overhead per month.

How Do You Calculate Overhead per Antique?

To be honest, antiques dealers do not and cannot add a specific, preset percentage above cost to each antique. Although most dealers in most types of retail shops do follow such a plan, they buy their merchandise from wholesalers at standard prices, add a standard markup percentage, and then sell the merchandise at standard prices.

For example, the owner of an auto parts store will buy a carton of twelve dozen spark plugs from a wholesaler for a standard catalog price, add his own specific markup, and then sell each spark plug for a standard price. He'll add the same markup percentage to batteries, radiator belts, and windshield wipers. The vendors he buys from will sell the same spark plugs, batteries, radiator belts, and windshield wipers to other auto parts dealers for the same wholesale prices, and the dealers will retail them to the public for approximately the same prices. So, the prices of those items will be fairly consistent throughout an industry.

Antiques dealers don't buy their antiques in large lots from wholesalers at standardized prices. Sometimes they come upon a great bargain and can easily price an antique at 200 percent, 300 percent, or even a higher percentage

> In setting your policies on prices, you have to consider the following:
>
> • what services you are offering
> • what your customers expect to pay
> • what the competition is charging
> • the area in which you live

above their costs. At other times they're lucky to get 75 percent above costs. Consequently, they don't figure on adding a preset percentage to each antique to cover their overhead. It just doesn't work that way. They simply try to price each antique so that the *average* markup will cover their overhead and give them a profit. Somehow, the ability to do this just seems to come naturally after a while. It's a combination of careful buying, research into current values, and experience in selling similar antiques.

In spite of this imprecise pricing system, most antiques dealers feel that they enjoy one of the best positions in retailing today, one that many other retailers can well envy. The reason? They and they alone are in complete control of the prices they place on their stock. No manufacturer sets the prices they must charge. Their antiques don't arrive on the shelf in a shiny cardboard box with a preprinted price and a bar code. Just as important, virtually everything in their shop is unique, one of a kind, so it's highly unlikely that any other shop in town will have an identical piece. Antiques dealers determine the prices they can charge to make a profit. To do this, you'll need to keep a close watch on your expenses, then price your individual antiques so that overall you'll show a profit.

Setting Your Prices

Economists, when counseling neophyte retailers about pricing, mention three philosophies open to them:

1. They can sell below the prevailing market prices for similar merchandise.
2. They can price their merchandise at approximately the same level as that of other dealers.
3. They can sell at prices above those of most other dealers.

So how can you, a home-based antiques dealer, apply these philosophies to your shop?

Pricing Below the Competition

This is a difficult policy to maintain for long and is seldom successful. Antiques dealers who work on a low profit margin must make up for the dollar loss by a high volume of sales combined with low overhead. Home-based antiques dealers who consistently follow this policy usually operate in the following way:

- They own their homes outright and have no mortgage payments. *Problem:* You may someday want to use such a property as collateral for a loan to expand your selling area. Then you would have payments to make. The best policy is to figure a mortgage payment into your overhead right from the first.
- They advertise only on special occasions such as annual sales. *Problem:* This is not good marketing. Statistically, the shop that advertises consistently draws customers. The one that doesn't advertise loses them.

- They plan on a fast turnover of their merchandise. *Problem:* This would be great if you could bank on it. But weather, a sluggish economy, changing tastes, or any number of other factors can mean occasional slow months for even the most successful shop.
- They buy only at very low prices. *Problem:* This is a fine practice if you can keep it up. Consistently paying rock-bottom prices, though, almost guarantees that you'll carry only low-grade antiques and collectibles. Customers looking for quality antiques (where the profit margin is nearly always higher) won't waste their time coming to your shop.
- They carry only low-priced antiques and collectibles. *Problem:* As above, you'll attract only customers looking for low-quality merchandise. In this business most dealers feel they must sell a few high-ticket antiques regularly to make a profit.
- They offer few or no services. This is not really a problem, as most customers of flea-market-type shops don't expect services.

Competitive Pricing

Competitive pricing means pricing at around the same level as that of other dealers in an area and is the policy of most dealers in antiques.

As a home-based dealer, you need to be constantly alert as to what other dealers *in similar locations and offering similar services* charge for their antiques. Visit other shops in your area regularly and check out their price tags. If you charge about the same prices, you should be able to maintain a steady clientele.

Pricing above the Competition

A policy of pricing above the competition is justified only when *nonprice* considerations are as important to your customers as quality merchandise. Here are some ways to attract customers willing to pay premium prices:

- Locate your shop/home in a relatively upscale neighborhood or give it the appearance of being exclusive. You can achieve an ambience of exclusivity with manicured landscaping and expensive exterior details, such as fancy brass light fixtures, brick walkways, and unusual building decor. Once inside your shop upscale customers may expect pleasant background music on a CD sound system, crystal chandeliers, uncrowded display areas, and a general sense of low-key merchandising.

- Stock antiques of exceptional quality and not usually available in other area shops. This means that you'll have to venture far beyond the sources—local auctions, estate sales, and so forth—that other local dealers use to purchase their stock. You also probably wouldn't stock as many items as does the owner of an average shop. Instead of ten $50 antique dolls, for example, you might display one $500 doll.
- Offer above-average services. Men and women who customarily patronize the finest shops expect leisurely assistance as they shop, free delivery, free trial-in-the-home, fine gift wrapping, colorful bags in which to carry their purchases home, off-street parking, and so forth. They are quite willing to pay premium prices to receive these services.

Regardless of which type of pricing schedule you plan to use, one rule is critical: The slower the turnover of merchandise, the higher the markup must be.

Figuring Markup Percentages

To calculate markup percentages (as shown on page 156), just divide the dollar markup on each antique by its selling price, and you'll get the markup percentage. Using the first item in the chart on page 156 as an example:

$39 (selling price) minus $12 (cost) = $27 (dollar markup)
$27 (dollar markup) divided by $39 (selling price) =
69% (markup percentage)

As long as the figures in the right column of your inventory records remain fairly consistent, you'll know that your buying and pricing practices are in the ballpark.

Why should you calculate percentage of markup rather than actual dollar markup? Because in many cases, percentages give you a better picture of which items will allow the largest markup, more so than simple dollar amounts. A quick glance down that column can show you almost immediately that you're making a better ratio of profit on pitchers and creamers than salt and peppers, for example. If this scenario is consistent, page after page in the record, you know not to go overboard in buying salt and peppers and to put more of your money in pitchers and creamers.

The percentages in the right column are not percentages of *profit*. They are *markup* percentages, which is a different story. Most dealers are happy to make a *profit* of 15 or 20 percent, which is what's left after all expenses or overhead are paid.

Good Research Means Successful Pricing

The most successful antiques dealers spend many hours every week researching current values so they'll know, almost instinctively, that an antique they come upon has the potential of making a profit for them. They pore over the annual price guides that list the selling prices of certain antiques nationwide. Like any annual reference book that's in use for an entire year, however, these guides list information that can easily go out of date if prices on certain antiques rise or fall drastically during that year.

Annual price guides usually reflect average prices on a *national* basis. Every astute dealer also reads the many *regional* papers that more accurately discuss trends and prices for specific areas of the country. As often as possible, they visit other antiques shops and attend antiques shows to determine how other dealers are pricing their merchandise. They sit through hours of auctions, watching what other dealers pay for antiques, knowing that those dealers will set prices of three, four, or five times their bids.

Here's an example of how you can make easy research pay off in a fast and profitable sale. Let's say you buy a Griswold iron pan at a yard sale for $1.00, knowing that Griswold is a hot item in the current collectibles market. Had you not, prior to the yard sale, studied the sections on Griswold ironware in your price guides, you might easily have overlooked the mark on the pan's bottom and passed it by. Once you have the pan home, you take a couple of minutes to research its specific current value. After checking the *Garage Sale &*

Sample China File

Code	Item	Cost	Price	Sold At	Date	% Markup
G71	Compote	$12	$39	$39	3/12	69%
G72	Plate	$4	$19	$19	4/22	79%
G73	Set/wines	$45	$129	$116	2/15	61%
G74	Set/goblets	$45	$98	$98	2/15	54%
G75	Pitcher	$3	$19	$19	2/15	84%
G76	Bottle	$ .50	$4	$4	6/3	87%
G77	Bottle	$ .50	$10	$10	6/3	95%
G78	Bottle	$ .50	$10	$9	8/10	94%
G79	Carafe	$10	$39	$35	5/14	71%
G80	Vase	$12	$19	$19	5/14	37%
G81	Vase	$5	$29	$24	4/22	79%
G82	Tray	$30	$79	$71	1/20	58%
G83	Lamp	$75	$250	$225	5/3	67%

Flea Market Annual, you find this particular pan listed at $75. So you place the pan in the shop at that price, and a collector snaps it up a few days later. This is a typical example of how constant study and research pay off in knowing not only what to buy but also how to price antiques.

Early on in your career as an antiques dealer, you'll probably miss some good buys simply because you hadn't done your research. For example, a dealer arrived at a yard sale just seconds ahead of another dealer, who was also a friend. As they browsed the tables of items, the first one passed by a small figurine, but the second quickly picked it up. The first dealer went on browsing. It wasn't until later, as they sat drinking coffee, that the second dealer asked the first, "Didn't you see that Goebel?"

"Goebel?" the first one asked.

The second dealer reached into her bag containing her purchases from the yard sale and brought out the figurine.

"This is a Goebel, made by the same company that produced the Hummel figurines. It's worth at least $60." She turned the little piece over and showed her friend the identifying mark. Needless to say, the first dealer went home and read up on Goebel pottery.

Planning Your Pricing Policy

One rule of thumb among most of the dealers I know is that you never buy an antique unless you can *at least* triple its cost to you when you place it in your shop. (Some dealers insist on paying no more than one-fifth of a reasonable selling price.) A markup of 65 percent is what it usually takes to cover overhead, markdowns, and mistakes and still make a profit.

A gentleman entered an antiques shop one spring day, wanting to sell a pair of especially nice mother-of-pearl opera glasses. The dealer offered him $50 for the glasses, knowing that she would probably be able to sell them for $150 when the fall theater season began. Until then, they would most likely sit in a display case, and the dealer's $50 investment would be tied up for six months. The man refused the dealer's offer, saying he'd seen a pair of opera glasses in a nearby shop for $125, and they were nowhere near the quality of his glasses. He thought the dealer should give him at least $100. So the dealer politely explained the realities of markup to him, and he said he understood. The dealer suggested that he try to sell the glasses to an individual. So the man walked out of the shop with the opera glasses in his pocket.

You'll encounter the same situation over and over as people bring you antiques they want to sell. Some will be as pleasant as the gentleman with the opera glasses. Some won't. You can suggest they run a classified ad in the local paper, for that's the only way they'll recover a price that's close to retail.

The exception to the rule of a minimum tripling of cost is with very high-priced

Pricing Antiques

Question: How do I know how to price my antiques?

Answer: Experienced dealers use four elements to help them set prices: authenticity, demand, condition, and restoration.

Authenticity. You should never take the authenticity of an antique for granted. For better-quality antiques, you should have a provenance or history of the piece, including who made it and who owned it, as well as notes on repairs or restorations. For more common pieces, marks or signatures will be enough, but furniture often doesn't have any. In establishing the authenticity of antiques that have been reproduced, like brass, china, glass, and furniture, much depends on your knowledge. You should closely examine any piece you buy for resale. Not only will this help you in deciding whether to buy it, but this will also help in pricing. The more knowledge you have about a particular piece, the more valuable it becomes to the collector. The more you know, the less danger there will be of your being taken in by a newer item being passed off as old.

Demand. As mentioned elsewhere in this book, buyers in different parts of the country look for and buy different types of antiques. An eighteenth-century French armoire that commands respect and a high price in New England might be passed up in New Mexico, where collectors usually look for antiques reflecting that area's Spanish heritage. Dealers consider the demand for an antique among local buyers.

Condition. Casual shoppers may not be too particular about a few scratches or a bit of rust on an antique. In contrast, serious collectors—those willing to pay the highest prices—demand top condition in the antiques they buy. For instance, assume that you have two plates of flow blue china in a desirable pattern but one has many knife scratches across its surface and the other is virtually scratch-free. The price tag on the second plate should be at least 30 percent higher than that on the first plate.

Restoration. Restored antiques and collectibles are pieces that have had breaks or lost parts repaired or replaced. This applies to furniture, china, and pottery, and sometimes to silver. To remain an antique, a piece should be 60 percent original. A "married" piece, made up of parts of two or more similar old pieces, is acceptable if the customer knows what he is buying. Any piece newly made of "old wood" or parts is still a reproduction. It's important that you take the amount or type of restoration into consideration when pricing your antiques.

antiques. You can then settle for a lower markup and still make a decent profit, especially if you know that one of your customers is a collector of that antique. For example, suppose you find an exquisite Oriental rug for which the seller wants $1,000. You know there's a collector in your town who will pay you $1,750 for it in a heartbeat, but he wouldn't pay $3,000. You buy the rug at $1,000, sell it two days later for $1,750, and make a tidy $750 profit.

What it boils down to is that antiques dealers set prices based on what's termed *demand-oriented pricing,* which means setting prices based on value, not cost, tempered by the vagaries of local tastes. Demand-oriented pricing with antiques works for two reasons: Antiques are unique, and they have intrinsic value, which is often in the eye of the customer. They're not standardized merchandise, identical tubes of toothpaste that can be found in every drugstore in town.

You may have three customers, for instance, who each desperately want a rosewood spool bed, but you can't simply pick up the phone and place an order with some distributor or wholesaler for three antique rosewood spool beds. You'll be lucky to find even one such bed. When you do come upon that one bed, which is a highly desirable antique, you'll price it accordingly, because you have three customers waiting for it. The demand is high.

This same principle keeps the prices of fine gems high. If diamonds were as common as rhinestones, the prices would be as low as those for rhinestones, but because diamonds are scarce and the demand for them is high, prices for diamonds are high, and people willingly pay those high prices.

The "You-Get-What-You-Pay-For" Syndrome

Since many antiques dealers begin their career selling at garage sales or flea markets, they acquire a flea-market mentality. That is to say, they're afraid to mark up quality items because no one will buy them, since patrons of these types of sales are looking for bargains. But professional antiques dealers, especially those who sell top-quality items, have a different philosophy. They believe that most customers won't respect an antique unless it has a decent price on it. If a dealer prices an item too low, the customer may think it's inferior or that it has a defect and will start looking for cracks or chips. Customers don't come into a nice antiques shop looking for great bargains. That's for flea markets. Collectors expect to pay a reasonable price for quality antiques. If you adopt this philosophy, you'll be able to make the profits that are possible in the antiques business.

You'll most likely become accustomed to buying low-priced collectibles and selling them at correspondingly low prices. And you'll be afraid to invest your money in better antiques that would bring higher prices, so you'll fill your shelves with merchandise that will bring only modest profits. Sooner or later you'll stumble upon and buy some excellent and highly desirable antiques. Even if you price them at their current high prices as listed in the antiques price guides, you'll be surprised at how fast they sell. At the same time, your inferior merchandise may sit on the shelves gathering dust. The lesson here is that people will pay for quality. If you cull the poor items and stock only antiques that bring decent prices, your profits will be correspondingly higher.

However, you have to be careful not to price yourself out of the market. The area in which you live determines to a large extent how much you can charge for your antiques. The owner of a shop in a trendy Baltimore neighborhood, for example, will be able to charge far more for a large stained-glass window than a dealer in Austin, Texas, can, regardless of how many people in that lovely western town want the window.

Your Services

Another element to consider when planning your pricing policy will be the services you'll offer. You'll have to factor many extras into your pricing system. One of the most valuable services you can give your customers actually costs you nothing—your extensive knowledge about antiques and the willingness to share that knowledge with them.

A recent survey by a New York public relations firm discovered that the shopping habits of many customers are changing. Fifteen or twenty years ago, price and quality influenced their purchases. Today's shoppers put more emphasis on service. They want to receive extensive information about their purchases from cheerful, well-informed salespeople. One executive put it this way: "People are no longer looking at price, price, price. Price was once the only criterion. Now it's not. They're looking for service."

You can put this trend in your favor if you develop a reputation for being the most knowledgeable and helpful dealer of antiques in your town. Take the time to educate your customers about styles of earlier periods. Show them how to gauge an antique's age. Share little anecdotes about history as it relates to antiques. These very personal services cost you absolutely nothing, but they're almost guaranteed to bring the customers flocking to your door.

Many other services you offer definitely will mean more expense for you and will have to be passed on in higher prices.

Delivery. Will you deliver furniture without charging for the service? Or will the price of the antique include delivery within a certain area, but you charge extra for delivery outside that area? Or will you have a flat no-delivery policy on everything, even a 10-foot-long dining table?

Layaway Plan. Will you have a layaway plan? You'll almost have to offer this service, since many customers simply can't pay the full price of an antique right upfront. The figure on page 162 is typical of a layaway contract. You keep a copy of this contract in your files and give the customer a copy. Note that each subsequent payment, after the down payment, is entered on the contract.

Any dealer who has a layaway plan learns pretty quickly the advantages and disadvantages of offering this service. First, the bad news: You won't lose any income by allowing a customer to pay off an antique in installments, but it does delay your receipt of the full amount of the purchase. Your money will be invested in the item, yet you don't realize your profit on it for perhaps ninety days. In the meantime, the antique is off the selling floor and you're losing the potential of selling it for immediate cash.

On the positive side, you'll increase your sales volume many times over by allowing customers to make a down payment on an antique, then pay off the balance in, say, three installments (the usual arrangement). The world is full of people who love antiques and sincerely want them for their homes but who must budget every dollar of their income. A layaway plan allows these people to allocate a few dollars every month in their budget to antiques. You'll make loyal customers of anyone who buys an antique from you on a layaway plan.

Checks. While it may seem obvious that if you're in business, you will accept checks for payment, many smaller antiques dealers are wary about accepting them. Though a check, even with proper identification, may seem like a sure method of payment, it's possible it will be returned unpaid for insufficient funds. The only hedge against this is either to not accept checks or to accept only those drawn on local banks.

Layaway Contract

Name _____

Address _____

Phone _____

Date _____

Antique to be put away on layaway _____

_____

Purchase price of antique _____

Down payment (minimum ⅓ of purchase price) _____

Note: Balance must be paid within 90 days. No refunds.

Purchaser's Signature _____

1st payment _____

Amount paid _____

2nd payment _____

Amount paid _____

3rd payment _____

Amount paid _____

Credit. Will you give credit—that is, allow a customer to take an antique or collectible and pay for it in monthly payments? Not unless the customer uses a credit card you accept. While you'll have to pay a small percentage of each purchase to the credit card company, this amount is worth it to let them handle any problems that may arise from nonpayment. Also, in today's retail market, accepting credit cards will attract more customers. By accepting credit cards—you must have a separate merchant account for each type of credit card you accept—you'll also attract your share of impulse buyers, who wouldn't make a purchase if they didn't carry a credit card.

Gift Wrapping/Elegant Packaging. Will you gift wrap? Few antiques shops offer this service, even for purchases that are intended as gifts. Will you have pretty bags printed with your shop's name, or will you use inexpensive plain ones from a wholesale paper firm? Plain bags will do nicely. After all, you're not competing with Tiffany—at least, not right now.

Think carefully about just how much you can afford to spend on anything except more antiques for your shop, especially in your first year as a dealer. Each expense must be passed on to your customers in higher prices.

Discounts

You also need to take into consideration the fact that most antiques dealers expect to get a 10 percent discount on anything they buy in the shop of another dealer. This is the usual courtesy dealers extend to one another. Many savvy customers who aren't dealers will also ask for a 10 percent discount on their purchases, and you're usually obligated to give these discounts. For this reason, many dealers automatically add 10 percent to the price they expect to get for an antique. But, remember, pricing up and then offering a discount, especially a substantial one, is dishonest. For example, take one dealer who constantly has 50-percent-off sales, but, in reality, has increased her prices over her already set ones before the sale. While some customers are naive enough to think they're getting a deal, they're actually paying full price for the item.

What about additional or larger discounts for special groups such as students and seniors? Few dealers regularly extend special discounts to such groups.

What do you do about the aggressive customer who picks up a pair of candlesticks you have priced at $79 and offers you $50 cash? It will happen. Do you stand firm at $79 or give in to make the sale, knowing you'll make some profit, even at $50? To be honest, this is demeaning. Would your customers go into a fine clothing shop, try on a half-dozen expensive gowns, and then haggle over the price of the prettiest one? Of course not. The shop owner would be horrified at such behavior. The reality of the antiques business, though, is that some customers will press you to lower your prices, even though you're not running a flea market, where haggling is expected.

Unfortunately, they equate "bargaining" with "antiques" and think they can bargain with any dealer.

Your policy about lowering prices should depend on two things:

1. How long has the antique been in your shop? Has it been sitting there for a year with virtually no interest from customers? In that case you'll probably be glad to get your investment back, plus at least a little profit.

    Let's say you bought a pretty framed needlework piece for $6.00 and placed it in your shop with a $39.00 price tag. Even though you thought it was well worth $39, it hung there on the wall for months. No one even looked at it. Finally, a customer offered you $25 for it. Without hesitation, you sold it to her. No, you didn't get its full value, but you then had $25 to invest in antiques that would move quickly.

2. How high was your original markup on the antique? If, after checking your records, you discover that you still will make a decent profit, even at the reduced price, you should go ahead and sell it. That was the case with the needlework piece. If you had paid $20.00 for it, you would not have let it go for $25.00, but at a cost to you of $6.00, you'll still come out ahead.

Odd-Ending Prices

Almost every drugstore, department store, and discount store uses the odd-ending pricing system—that is, merchandise is priced at $3.98 or $3.95 instead of $4.00. The reason is psychological. Many customers tend to mentally round down a $3.98 price tag to $3.00. However, just as many others round it up to $4.00. Odd-ending, though, has never been a practice in most quality antiques shops.

Some dealers feel that odd-ending of pennies cheapens the value of an antique. After all, you're selling investment, beauty, and pleasure, not cornflakes. Yet odd-ending of dollars doesn't seem to have the same devaluing effect. Pricing your antiques at $19, $39, $149, and so forth can be quite effective. Some dealers round their prices off at $15, $25, $100, and so forth. There's no right or wrong here. Just make your own decision based on your own feelings about pricing.

Multiple and Individual Pricing

How do you price antiques that come in sets: chairs, crystal and china, sterling silver flatware, and so forth? Do you write one price tag that covers the entire set, or do you price each unit individually? It depends.

Chairs. If you have a set of six matching chairs, for instance, price them at six for one figure. The reason is that most people will want all six chairs. Very few customers will be trying to find one chair to complete a set they already own. Craftspersons of generations ago used literally thousands of patterns in the furniture they constructed, so the chances of your having duplicates of a customer's chairs are almost astronomically impossible. Besides, if you sold one chair from your set, you'd be left with just five chairs, a partial set.

Crystal and China. Crystal and china, especially if they're of a fairly popular pattern, are a different story. You'll seldom find a complete set of crystal or china. The very nature of old china and crystal is that a few pieces would have been broken through the years. As a result, many of your customers will own partial sets, and they're always cruising the antiques shops looking for an odd piece or two to help fill out the set.

What if you found a set of antique china? Though it was originally a service for twelve, plus covered tureens, platters, a gravy boat, and vegetable dishes, when you bought it it also contained twelve berry bowls and twelve soup plates. However, it had only nine dinner plates, eleven luncheon plates, ten bread-and-butter plates, and nine cups and saucers, two of which were chipped. You would be constantly on the lookout for odd pieces to bring it back to its original service for twelve. If by some miracle you came upon a full set in a shop, you certainly wouldn't want to buy the whole thing, but you would buy individual pieces in a minute.

Most dealers find it simply easier to sell each piece of a partial china set separately rather than as a whole. In the end they'll make more profit. But this is limited to only certain antiques and collectibles, such as pottery, porcelain, and silver. You can certainly extend this policy by offering a slightly discounted price to a customer who buys all of the pieces of a certain pattern in your shop. If there are only a few pieces of a pattern, you should price them individually, especially if the pattern is difficult to find.

Sterling Silver Flatware. If you're lucky enough to obtain a complete set of antique sterling silver flatware, never break it up because collectors highly value a complete set.

Don't hesitate to buy and display odd pieces of the more popular patterns, though. As with crystal, many people are always searching for a spoon here, a fork there to fill out a set.

Groups of Odd Items. Many times you'll have small items in your shop that simply don't warrant your time in pricing them individually. That's when you group them and sell them as one unit. For instance, a dealer bought three big fruit jars full of old marbles. About twenty of the marbles were valuable enough to be priced separately at $5.00 each. The remaining ones were worth from $1.00 to $2.00 each, so he placed twenty-five of these in each of eight plastic bags and priced them at $29.00 a bag. This saved him the time he would have spent pricing each marble separately and the trouble of selling them one or two at a time. Buyers got a bargain in that they received twenty-five collectible marbles for less than the cost of buying them separately.

Hard-to-Price Items. As time goes on, you may acquire a library of reference books on everything from autographs to zithers but still not be able to locate a reasonable selling price for an unusual antique you come upon. In that case you call a local dealer who handles *current* merchandise similar to your antique and ask him the price of a top-of-the-line piece. Use that figure as your guideline.

You may have to use this technique when you come across an item, say, a 1930s Wilson tennis racquet in superb condition, that you can't find in any of your reference books. In this case you need to call a local sporting goods shop and ask the price of its best Wilson tennis racquet. Usually, the shopkeeper will cheerfully give you the figure, and you'll be able to price your racquet accordingly, since highly collectible items often sell for as much as new ones of the same type.

This technique also comes in handy when you need to identify the pattern of a particular piece of sterling, crystal, or china. Whenever possible, you'll find it to your advantage to list pattern names on your price tags because many patterns are incredibly similar. No customer wants to buy a wine glass or sterling fork, for example, and then discover, once he gets home, that it's similar to but not exactly his pattern.

One way you can identify a pattern is to take the piece—whether it's sterling, china, or crystal—to a local jewelry or china shop and ask the manager if it is illustrated in one of the shop's catalogs. You may find a photograph of the piece there, along with the pattern name and retail price.

Price Tags

You'll need many thousands of price tags, even in your first year of business. Small stringed tags are fine for small items such as cups and saucers, but you may tag your medium-to-large antiques using your business cards. Since you're going to buy business cards anyway, simply increase your order to 5,000 or so.

Any good copy center can print 5,000 business cards for about a penny each. Order them in a color and type style that coordinates with your street sign and advertising. Include on the cards the name of your shop, your address and phone number, and your logo, if you've chosen one.

To convert these business cards into price tags, first punch a hole in the upper-left corner of a card, using a standard hole punch. Cut about a foot of yarn or narrow ribbon in a coordinating color and thread it through the hole. Write the price of the antique on the card below or to the side of your shop's name or on the reverse side, and tie the card, using the attached yarn or ribbon, to the antique. You now have an attractive price tag that's highly visible and that remains as an advertisement of your shop after the customer takes the antique home.

You're probably thinking, *"Punch holes in thousands of cards? Cut and tie yarn through thousands of holes? Yikes!"* The secret is to start as early as possible, building up a supply before you ever open your shop. Draft your friends and family to help. You'll need a continual supply of these tags after you open the shop, too, so just prepare a few more every day during slow periods. You'll always have plenty of attractive price tags on hand this way.

Some of your antiques, such as bowls, vases, and most china, won't lend themselves to tie-on tags. For those pieces most dealers just use the self-adhesive labels that come in packages of 1,000. Don't buy any labels smaller than ½ inch by ¾ inch. You need room to write the antique's code number along with its price, and the very tiny ones aren't large enough.

Never stick an adhesive price tag on paper goods. This includes prints, sheet music, books, postcards, playing cards, and so forth. Old paper is fragile, and many adhesive tags will effectively remove printing or even the paper itself when the tag is removed. Far too many holes in paper goods are made when some dealer had stuck a tag on them, essentially ruining the collectible.

The best solution is to drop the item into a plastic sleeve, then stick the price tag on the sleeve. You can order plastic sleeves in many sizes, ranging all the way from some large enough to hold sheet music down to little ones just right for the smallest postcards. Suppliers of these plastic sleeves advertise in trade journals.

To a certain extent the same caveat about sticking adhesive labels on paper goods holds true for linens. Many times an adhesive tag will leave a residue on a fine linen handkerchief, for example, that's almost impossible to remove. Write the price on a small string tag, then pin the tag to the linen with a tiny safety pin. Buy little brass pins in bags of one hundred at a crafts store.

It isn't practical to put books in plastic bags customers like to browse through them, and you can't stick safety pins in books. But you might want to try this: Open the book to its approximate center, then place a piece of yarn about 2½ feet long along the channel between pages. Close the book; then take the two ends of the yarn and tie them securely along the book's outer spine. Tie a string tag to the knot in the yarn, tie the ends of the yarn into a bow, then cut off all excess yarn. This creates a secure and attractive price tag that won't come off even when customers flip through the book.

SOLD Tags

Every once in a while you'll sell an antique, usually a large piece of furniture, that the customer can't take home right away. It has to stay on the sales floor for a while. That's a perfect time to make a real statement to your other customers about the salability of your antiques. All you have to do is tie a large red tag that blazons SOLD onto the antique and let it sit there in plain view. This not only informs customers that your antiques are selling, but it lets them know that they shouldn't hesitate if they're genuinely interested in an antique. It might not be there when they come back.

A dealer once had for sale a late-nineteenth-century secretary that carried a fairly high price. One day a woman and her husband came in his shop, saw the desk, and fell in love with it. They came back several times, examining the piece, measuring it, discussing how it would fit into their home. She really wanted the secretary but just couldn't make up her mind to buy it. Early one Saturday morning, someone else purchased the secretary, but the customer had to leave it in the shop for a few days. So the dealer put a SOLD tag on it. That afternoon the woman's husband came in with a fistful of hundred-dollar bills, ready to buy the secretary as a surprise birthday gift for his wife. He almost went into shock when he saw that SOLD tag. Unfortunately, that's how the antiques buying game works. Since a dealer usually has only one of the item, when it sells, it's gone. As the old saying goes, "He who hesitates is lost."

Try to impress this thought on your customers: If they see an antique they like, they should buy it right then (or put it on layaway), because it may not be there when they come back. Those red SOLD tags are all the evidence you need to make your point.

Markdowns and Sales

In certain types of businesses, retailers price their merchandise high enough to accommodate substantial markdowns at the end of a season. They plan ahead on taking reductions because they know that statistically they'll have leftover merchandise then. They also know that they may overbuy on certain items or sizes—too many size 40 jackets or purple bikinis, for example. They may stock up on flowered sheets just before the decorating magazines begin promoting striped sheets.

These problems don't exist in the antiques business, which is not to say dealers don't ever reduce the price on an antique. They just don't do it very often and certainly not on the scale of most retail shops.

There isn't an antiques dealer who hasn't paid too much for an antique or bought something that turned out to be a real dog in some way. If such an antique sits in their shop for a year or more with absolutely no response from customers, the only solution is to reduce the price, sell it, and get it out of the shop. Better to take a loss than to have your customers become bored looking at the same tired merchandise.

Periodically, many dealers find themselves with stock that they feel was a mistake to buy and that they just want to get out of their shop. Conducting regular sales is usually the best way to get rid of this merchandise.

Suppose, however, for whatever reason, you want to place some antiques on sale between regular sales. It doesn't hurt to attach sale tags to a few items, certainly. But don't make the mistake of tying too many red sale tags onto items around your shop. Customers may think you're going out of business.

Group a number of sale items on one table in a corner of the shop. Though the table probably won't hold everything you've tagged, as pieces sell fill the spaces with other tagged items. You'll find customers are actually drawn to the sale table, looking for bargains.

Most dealers don't simply cross out the original price and write in a lower price, however. They create an entirely new price tag with the new, lowered price. This practice has a two-pronged benefit.

First, a few unscrupulous shoppers will, unfortunately, mark through the price on a tag and claim that it was reduced by the dealer. It's hard to deny such a claim if other tags are so marked, but if you never change the prices yourself on tags, customers won't be able to do so, either.

Second, customers who look at a new price tag see an antique with a low price, not one that you lowered. Psychologically, this is better for your business. Marked-over prices give the impression your antiques aren't selling.

Many shops do have regular sales, though, usually in early spring and late fall. Some do quite well with this practice. Of course, you'll always have customers who wait for these sales. They've had their eyes on certain antiques for weeks or months, hoping to get the piece at a reduced price. So be it. You'll still make a decent profit on those sales.

Instead of marking new prices on existing tags, however, you can place several signs around that state 15% OFF EVERY ANTIQUE IN THE SHOP. This way, when the sale—usually of two weeks' duration—is over, you won't have to write and attach new tags. Everything just automatically goes back to the original price.

Other dealers prefer to lower the prices on certain antiques but not on others. They either mark sale prices on the old tags or group the sale antiques on specific tables or in specific areas.

You might decide to hold an annual yard sale of marked-down antiques and collectibles. Close your home-based shop for a Saturday morning and put all your sale items out on the front lawn. This keeps customers from thinking everything in the shop is on sale. At noon close out the yard sale, open your shop, and you're right back in business.

Is there a flea market in operation anywhere near your home? If so, selling off your mistakes there is another way to recoup some or all of your investment and get the unsalable items out of the shop. Hundreds of bargain-hunting men and women crowd the aisles of these open-air markets. The exposure is terrific, so the effort put into hauling the leftovers there and spending a day selling them can pay off handsomely. The rent for tables at flea markets is usually quite reasonable, so even though you reduce the prices on your mistakes to rock-bottom, you'll still come home with money in your pocket to invest in new stock.

Selling Seasonal Items

Many dealers like to add seasonally oriented antiques to their regular display for special occasions—Christmas, Easter, June (weddings), and so forth. This practice does, however, present the problem of what to do with the pieces that don't sell once the season has passed. Should you reduce their prices to recoup some of your investment, or should you store them for the following year?

Some feel high-ticket items should be stored. Low-priced stock, however, just takes up valuable space if it has to be stored for an entire year.

During the winter holiday season, a dealer had several pieces of china, each with a Christmas motif. Virtually all of it sold except one cup and saucer, priced at $12. On the day after Christmas, a woman offered her $4.00 for the set. She politely refused the offer, since that was exactly what she had invested in the set and would therefore make no profit on such a sale.

Later it dawned on her that she'd made a mistake. Even though she would have made no profit, at $4.00 she would have recouped what she paid for the cup and saucer and been able to invest the money in something else immediately. As it was, she had to wrap and store the two pieces and wait a whole year for another chance to sell them.

Markdown Inventory

One way to avoid making future mistakes in buying is to keep a running record of every antique whose price you must reduce (see the following page). This record is in addition to your inventory and sales records. Record each marked-down antique, what you paid for it, the original tagged price, and the final selling price. By studying this record, you'll know either not to buy such antiques in the future or not to invest too much money in them. Another copy of this form is in the appendix.

A Checklist for Profitable Pricing

Before you price your stock of antiques, study the following checklist carefully:

- ☐ Have you surveyed or studied your area to determine the prices charged by other antiques shops?
- ☐ Have you determined at what price level you plan to operate your shop: below, at, or above the competition?
- ☐ Have you made arrangements for all the services you will offer your customers?
- ☐ After estimating your sales volume and overhead, have you calculated what your average markup will be?
- ☐ Have you established a policy on discounts?
- ☐ Have you established a policy on odd-ending and multiple pricing?
- ☐ Will you keep records of all merchandise that must be reduced in price?
- ☐ Have you established a policy on when and how much to mark down antiques that don't sell?

Markdown Inventory

Code #	Item	Purchase Price	Original Price	Sale Price

Chapter Eight

Display and Merchandising

Good planning, an attractive shop, salable merchandise, and top-notch marketing function as a team with one goal—to bring customers to your shop. Once customers are in the door, you'll use two additional powerful aids to make them say the magic words, "I'll take it!" These two helpers are *enticing displays* and *effective merchandising*.

The way you display your antiques and the way you present them to your customers are crucial to your success as an antiques dealer. They're the little extras that are like icing on cake, whipped cream on Irish coffee, extra topping on pizza. The good news is that it's easier to master creative display techniques and skillful merchandising than just about any other facet of managing an antiques shop.

Displaying Your Antiques

Creating an Image

The research you conducted for your business plan helped you understand pretty well who your customers will be as well as their income level, shopping habits, and preferences as to the types of antiques they might choose for their homes. You used this information as you stocked your shop. Now you'll use the same information in displaying your antiques. Since you know what merchandise your customers expect to find when they visit your shop, you'll create and maintain an image in your displays that harmonizes with their expectations. With one big exception (you'll read about it in Chapter 10), the person who enters a *home-based antiques shop* is not expecting to walk in under Waterford crystal chandeliers and to be offered a glass of fine champagne to sip as she shops. She'll probably be more comfortable in a casual, informal atmosphere, one that feels like home.

A big advantage you have over owners of shops in commercial space is that your antiques actually are displayed in a home. Play that up in every way you can.

Types of Displays

Displays usually fall into one of three categories: open, closed, or ledge. Each of these categories has a specific use.

1. *Open displays* are those that are scattered throughout the shop and are easy for the customer to inspect. They include furniture, small antiques displayed on furniture, and open shelves. Most dealers consider this the ideal type of display. It's just human nature, of shoppers, anyway, to want to inspect any item that interests them. The very act of reaching out to an antique, picking it up, looking underneath, holding it to the light, and then reading the price tag often leads to the decision to buy. You can't discount the value of easy access in merchandising antiques.

This same easy access, however, can lead to breakage or damage. Some parents don't watch their children as closely as they should, and every antiques

Customers will frequently pick up a small antique and carry it around with them as they shop. In most cases, they're simply holding on to the piece while they decide whether to buy it. Yet some dealers have lost a few valuable antiques to shoplifters who'll do just that, then drop it into a handbag or pocket when the dealers are not looking and leave while they're busy with other customers.

You don't want to offend perfectly honest customers by implying that they're about to shoplift something. The best solution seems to be to approach the customer with a smile and say, "Would you like for me to put that [perfume bottle, bag of marbles, bowl, or whatever] at the counter for you so you don't have to carry it around while you shop?"

This friendly request never irritates anyone.

dealer alive has cringed as an overexuberant child knocked a piece of fine porcelain into history. One especially short-fused dealer posted a sign in his shop warning UNACCOMPANIED CHILDREN WILL BE SOLD TO GYPSIES! Now that was a bit much, but for some reason mothers of small children would read the sign, laugh, then grab their little darlings' hands and hold on for dear life. Maybe that dealer had something, after all.

2. *Closed displays* are glass cases, usually locked, and are the alternative to open displays. They're the place for valuable, fragile, or small antiques. Do antiques sell as well in closed displays as on open shelves? No. Somehow, a pane of glass creates a psychological as well as a physical barrier between the customer and the antique. It intimidates all but those who are seriously interested in a piece. A customer who is only mildly interested in an antique displayed on an open shelf will still pick it up to read the price tag. However, she usually won't ask a busy shop owner to unlock a case to inspect the same antique. Nevertheless, this is the only reasonable alternative for some antiques, especially very small items.

    Aside from breakage, you have to consider the possibility of theft. *Never* display genuinely valuable small antiques or any type of jewelry, even marginally collectible pieces, on open shelves. Unfortunately, shoplifters find it too easy to scoop them into a pocket or shopping bag. Such pieces must go into a closed and locked case.

    A dealer learned this lesson the hard way after a shoplifter made off with two sterling silver souvenir spoons she had placed in a spoon rack hanging on a wall. He also stole several pieces of 1940s jewelry that were lying on a velvet-covered tray on top of a case. Better to miss a few questionable sales than lose good merchandise to shoplifters. Any customer who is genuinely interested in an antique will ask to have a case opened.

3. *Ledges* are windowsills, the tops of cabinets or dividers, or any flat surface (other than a shelf) where merchandise can be displayed. Ledges are great areas for relatively inexpensive but attractive antiques and collectibles. They're the ideal places to put pieces that will draw customers from one area of a shop to another, often out of curiosity.

    Perhaps you have twenty-five or thirty unusual purple and blue bottles that you can cluster on a sunny windowsill grouped by color. On a bright day this display can be most attractive, both from the inside of the shop and from outside. Or maybe you have some dainty handkerchiefs that you can arrange in a small basket to set on a table in your shop. Customers will pause in their browsing to look through the basket. If they decide to buy one, fine. The important point, though, is that they stopped in that area for a few minutes.

The most valuable ledge is the top of your glass case. You could place an attractive teapot, small lamp, or colorful cup and saucer there to attract attention. Customers will be drawn to the antique on top of the case and may stay to investigate the sterling silver, perfume bottles, and miniatures displayed *inside* the case.

Effective Lighting

Take advantage of light to help display your antiques. You can add a romantic, old-fashioned charm to your inventory by placing several lamps, fitted with decorative iridescent flamelike 40-watt bulbs, throughout the shop. Your customers, who use incandescent bulbs in their own homes, will find the pools of warm golden light from these bulbs cheerful and inviting as they brighten dull corners and highlight choice pieces of furniture. This light is also flattering to a woman's complexion—especially important when she's trying on jewelry or vintage clothing—and is perfect to illuminate the patina of your antique furniture.

Incandescent light bulbs, however, are expensive to buy and operate, and unless you use a great many high-wattage bulbs, they won't keep your shop effectively lighted. The heat from many 100-watt incandescent bulbs, too, can be disastrous if your shop is not air-conditioned. The solution to this situation is to use a combination of low-wattage incandescent bulbs for charm and high-wattage fluorescent tubes for light. As you know, fluorescent tubes are highly energy-efficient and give off a great deal of light per dollar spent. Considering the current cost of electricity, they are a bargain. On the downside, however, long, industrial-looking tubes don't do a thing for the ambience of an antiques shop. In fact, they look pretty awful. The secret is to hide them.

When you remodel your home to accommodate your antiques shop, you might consider having valances built around all the walls at the ceiling line. An electrician can wire the wall for fluorescent tubes, which can then be hidden behind the valances. The light from the tubes will be directed up and onto the ceiling, where it will diffuse and spread around the room. The light will illuminate the entire room with no sharp shadows. Fluorescent tubes come in several tones, ranging from cool to warm. Be sure to buy the warmest ones. Their color will blend nicely with the warm tones of the incandescent bulbs.

Do you have large windows facing the street? If so, keep some of your lamps lit during the evening hours so that your showroom is visible to passersby. Many times a customer will return to inspect an antique she glimpsed through a window the previous night.

Make Color Work for You

Color sells! There's a psychology to color that can't be denied.

- *Red* is exciting, powerful, sexy, patriotic. It can also be disturbing. Use it in moderation.
- *Yellow* is cheerful and happy, signifying youth and energy. It's great when used against a dark background.
- *Blue* symbolizes water and sky, peace and serenity. It's also men's favorite color, so use it wherever you want to attract male customers.
- *Green* is fresh and cool, like forests and the great outdoors. When teamed with yellow, it says "Spring."
- *Pink* is sweet and lovely, innocent and young. Coordinate pink with lace and ribbons for Mother's Day and June brides.

Many people dislike purple and are depressed by gray, so you might think twice about using them in your displays. Orange, too, is disturbing to some people, so avoid it (except for Halloween).

Keep color in mind as you set up your displays. A few pieces of colored glass scattered around a room won't attract much attention. *Group* them by color, however, and you multiply the impact many times over. For example, place a half-dozen blue canning jars on a Hoosier cabinet, a collection of green Depression glass on a dining table, and several pieces of ruby-colored glass on a white marble-topped table.

Do you have a framed print that depicts a bowl of colorful flowers? You could emphasize those colors as well as the beauty of the picture by creating an interesting tableau before it. Perhaps a cup and saucer, teapot, and pretty vase, all in colors that harmonize with the flowers, would do the trick.

One successful dealer uses lengths of fabric lavishly as backdrops for her antiques, and every piece of cloth is especially chosen for color and texture. She'll place rare old duck decoys on a piece of greenish brown fabric that looks for all the world like the water of a lake. She'll cover a round table with a delicate pink cloth to highlight a set of rose-sprigged china. Jetblack glass candlesticks stand on a swath of stark white cloth to emphasize their color. Be careful when choosing the fabrics you use alongside your antiques, though. Some colors just don't mix. Most old china, for example, slightly yellowed with age, looks plain dingy when placed on the same snow-white cloth that makes the candlesticks appear so elegant.

Think color, too, when decorating for a holiday. Your customers will love seeing a collection of green accessories around St. Patrick's Day; red and white for Valentine's Day; red, white, and blue for July Fourth; orange and black for Halloween; and red and green for Christmas.

Display Props

Props are any physical objects that you use to display an antique but that aren't salable merchandise in themselves. Employ props to make an antique more visible, to enhance its color or style, or to draw attention to it. (The fabrics mentioned in the preceding section are really props.) A prop doesn't overshadow or detract from the antique. It enhances the antique without drawing undue attention to itself.

Some excellent commercial props are advertised in the various antiques trade papers. These props include small Lucite boxes that can be used to raise an antique a few inches off a shelf, plate holders, cup-and-saucer holders, and doll stands.

The most interesting props, though, are those you'll find for little or no cost. Going to the coast on vacation? Look for pretty shells to display your pearl jewelry. Interesting driftwood is great to use around any nautical antique. A battered bucket that surfaces behind a relative's barn could be scrubbed, painted, and used to hold piano rolls. Old bricks, with their soft rust color and appealing texture, might serve to display antique tools. You could use an old crate to hold used collectible magazines or small prints. Many dealers display odd plates and platters in folding wooden dish drainers.

Of course, you can also use antiques or collectibles to display other antiques. For instance, hang an embroidered tea towel on the upper bar of a little washstand or stack old spice cans on top of a bread box or rest an old doll or teddy bear on a high chair. These aren't really props, though, since you intend to sell them.

Positioning Your Antiques

Think Proportion and Balance. When an artist first sketches the design for a painting, she considers proportion and balance—how the various elements will relate to one another. You should do the same before positioning your antiques. Here are some general rules:

- Curving or diagonal lines are more interesting than straight lines.
- Asymmetrical groupings are more interesting than symmetrical ones, and elements of varying sizes are more interesting than those of identical sizes.
- *Three* seems to be a magic number in design, one that implies harmony. These three elements might be three different sizes, three different heights, or three different colors.

As you position your antiques, look for ways to use curving or diagonal lines, elements of different sizes, and units of three elements in your displays.

You don't have this much freedom when displaying antiques on a bank of shelves, of course. Even so, you can create interest by using antiques of differing sizes or by placing some things close to the wall and others forward.

Not long ago a dealer set up a special display of about thirty-five sets of cups and saucers in preparation for Mother's Day. He placed them on two glass shelves, then stood back to evaluate the display. It was awful! The dealer thought he had done it properly because he used a zigzag pattern, placing one set forward and the next set back. The display was totally boring because there was no variation in height. Fortunately, the solution was easy. He placed the sets that were in the rear on cup-and-saucer holders. This arrangement gave some height to the display, as well as making the sets in the rear more visible.

Group Your Antiques for Maximum Effect. The way you group your antique furniture can help your customers visualize it in their own homes. Many people who come into your shop will be searching for a specific item. They may need a table to place beside a couch, a

Displaying Large Furniture

Question: How can I use the elements of proportion and balance to highlight a large piece of furniture?

Answer: Let's assume you have a mahogany buffet that's 36 inches high and 54 inches wide, and has a flat top.

You might hang a large picture (24 inches square) on the wall above the left end of the buffet; that's element 1 in height and size. You could stand a few old books (8 inches high) in the center of the buffet; that's element 2 in height and size. On the far right side of the buffet, you could place a delicate chocolate pitcher (12 inches high) surrounded by a few cups; that's element 3 in height and size.

This arrangement uses the curving line principle, from top left down to center and up to the right. The grouping is also asymmetrical, since the picture is larger and higher than the chocolate set.

pie safe to hold their VCR and tapes, or a floor lamp to use as a reading light. Arrange your antique furniture in casual groupings, just as they might be in a home, so that your customers can actually see, for example, the way a low table might serve as a coffee table, especially if you place an attractive candy bowl or a few books on it.

If you specialize in one period (eighteenth century, Victorian, primitive, and so forth), you'll have no trouble displaying your antique furniture in such groupings. If, like most dealers, you carry antiques of several eras, try not to display, all in one corner, a turn-of-the-century Bible table with an Art Nouveau floor lamp and a red velvet sofa right out of *Gone with the Wind*. This creates instant confusion.

The trick is to group antiques of specific eras together. In one room or alcove, you might place formal, English antiques, along with appropriate accessories. In another section of the shop, display antiques of another style or period. This system not only adds to the harmony of your decor but also helps customers as they search for that special antique. The person who wants a Hoosier cabinet will be immediately drawn to your "country" display, whereas the one looking for an Eastlake table for her late-nineteenth-century bed-room will gravitate quickly to the area filled with Victorian antiques.

The same theory holds true for collectibles. Group them according to category. If you have several nice Coca-Cola pieces, for example, display them in one area. Then, if a collector comes into the shop searching for Coca-Cola items, she'll be drawn immediately to that display. If you scatter a Coca-Cola tray here and a bottle carrier there throughout the shop, intermingled with every other kind of collectible, she could easily overlook a few choice items—and you might miss a sale!

Keep 'Em Moving!

One final word about displays: Rearrange your antiques regularly. Shift furniture from one side of the room to another. Put cookie jars in a bookcase one month and on a library table the next. Move cups and saucers from a shelf on one wall to a shelf on another wall. This is one of the best ways to keep your regular customers from becoming bored with your stock.

Sometimes an antique will look completely different in one setting from the way it does in another. You'll be amazed at how rearranging your stock can create interest and generate sales. It's axiomatic among dealers that regular customers can walk right by an antique a dozen times and never see it. Move it to another location and they say, "Oh, there's the lamp I've been seeking for months!"

Suppose you have an antique that hasn't sold despite moving it all over the shop. You feel strongly that the piece is worth the price you placed on it, so you don't want to mark it down. In this case it's time to remove it from the shop for a breather. Take it off the shelf or floor, store it for three or four months, then bring it back out. The chances are that even your regular customers won't recognize the piece, and it'll look like new stock to them.

A dealer had a problem selling an old Raggedy Ann cookie jar. At the time she first placed it on a shelf, she priced it as listed in all the reference books. For some reason it didn't sell, even though it was a desirable collectible and fairly priced. After six months, she took it down and stored it. Once back on the shelf, *at the same price,* that cookie jar sold within a week.

Merchandising Your Antiques

Hard Selling Is for Used Cars—Soft Selling Is for Antiques

Antiques buyers are browsers. Unless they've been in the shop before and have already chosen a particular antique, they like to wander around at their leisure. Most of them sincerely resent having a salesperson on their heels, loudly heralding the value of every antique that even casually catches their attention. This is the fastest way to antagonize a potential customer and chase her out of the shop. The soft sell—low-key, laid-back, friendly but not aggressive—is the most effective way to sell antiques.

This isn't to say that you should ignore your customers. Far from it. The best method, according to most antiques dealers, is to greet *each* customer with a friendly "Hello, there" when she walks into the shop. You can follow that with "Let me know if I can answer any questions or help you with anything." If your customers indicate that they're looking for specific items, you should try to find what they're asking for among your inventory. However, if they say, "I'm just looking around," you can smile warmly and say, "Go right ahead." Then make yourself busy with some small task, while staying alert to any questions they might have.

Be sure to acknowledge each customer, even if you're busy with one person when another enters. You can still glance in the newcomer's direction, smile, give her a pleasant greeting, and then go back to helping the first person.

Should you be suddenly rushed with a half-dozen or more customers, announce in a voice just loud enough to be heard by all, "Look around, folks; I'll be with you in a minute." This announcement makes them feel welcome, and they'll most likely stay in the shop until you can get to them. Otherwise, they might walk out, sensing that you're too busy to wait on them.

Most successful dealers wait until a customer shows a real interest in a specific antique before making an effort to sell it. At that point, though, you can begin merchandising. "The inlay on that cabinet is so delicate and intricate. See how the cabinetmaker used ivory and mother-of-pearl to create the pattern?" Or "I see you're interested in the Frankoma pottery. Are you a collector? If you'll notice the color of the clay on the bottom of these pieces, you'll see they're all from the first firings."

If customers leave the shop without buying, send them on their way with just as much warmth as you showed when they entered. "Thanks for stopping by! And please visit us again." In any event, whether they buy or not, encourage all customers to sign your guest register. You want those names and addresses for your mailing list.

Sell the Sizzle, Not the Steak

All right, you know you're not in the restaurant business, but when Elmer Wheeler, a very cagey fellow, told a group of salesmen, "Don't sell the steak, sell the sizzle," he made merchandising history. That truism works in any business, including antiques. You sell the *benefits* of owning an antique, not the antique itself.

After all, a table is a table is a table, to misquote Gertrude Stein. A table is four legs and a flat top. As an antiques dealer, are you selling your customers four legs and a flat top? No. You're selling beauty, prestige, investment, pleasure, and pride of ownership.

Show a customer how the deep patina on an Empire-era table enhances the wood and she'll immediately see it glowing in her own home. Explain how the table's lines reflect Napoléon's influence on French architecture and furniture and she can relate the table to that period in history. Show that such a table is quite rare, and she'll realize she's buying a piece of furniture that's one of a kind, a genuine asset to her collection. Let her see how the table's simple yet elegant lines will complement the other furniture in her living room, creating an arrangement that will evoke admiration from all who see it.

In other words, get your customers' *emotions* involved. Instead of seeing merely a set of pretty Meissen china, let a woman visualize how she might set her table with the china, then invite friends over for a festive dinner. Let her imagine the pleasure she'll derive every time she looks at the lovely pattern. Maybe she'll even be able to pass the set on to a daughter or son. That's selling the sizzle, not the steak!

Look for the Stories Behind Your Antiques

As you buy stock for your shop, try to find out whether an antique has an interesting history. This isn't always possible, of course, but surprisingly often when you buy from individuals, they can tell you fascinating stories about their marble-topped tables, cut-glass cruets, hobnail perfume bottles, or whatever. Maybe it's a canteen carried by a soldier during the Spanish-American War. Or it might be a Bible brought through Ellis Island by an immigrant from Ireland. It could be an old maple rocking chair that survived the long trek on the Oregon Trail. Perhaps it's a fanciful cane that once belonged to your state's most revered governor.

Any such history adds much to the value of an antique when you describe it to a customer. Stories are also *invaluable* to someone who collects that particular type of antique.

Suppose someone comes into your shop asking for button hooks that carry advertising slogans from shoe shops. If you happen to have an advertising-related button hook that you can pretty well document as having belonged to Lizzie Borden, Emily Dickinson, Annie Oakley, or some other famous woman, you can be certain that collector will pay you a premium price for it. For this reason, ask the seller of an especially interesting antique, "Can you tell me something about this?"

Granted, you have to take some tales with a grain of salt if they sound too fanciful. After all, what are the chances of a sea chest that came over on the *Mayflower* being found in a rancher's tack room in Wyoming? Pretty slim. Just use your judgment, based on the credibility of the seller.

Accentuate the Positive

No one likes a Gloomy Gus, yet too many dealers can't resist peppering their conversation with dire comments about the state of the economy, the world, and everyone in it. They don't like the politicians in Washington or the way the last election went. According to them, their competition is selling inferior merchandise. On and on and on. Who can blame a potential customer for getting out of that shop as quickly as possible?

Enthusiasm and a positive attitude have to be two of the greatest assets an antiques dealer can project, and the enthusiasm you feels for your profession is contagious. When you act as though each antique in your shop is a thing of joy and beauty, your customers will begin to see them as such, and they can't help but respond. Your happy attitude will rub off on your customers, and they'll be much more likely to buy.

Chapter Nine

Marketing: Letting the World Know You're Here

You know you have a good selection of antiques and collectibles, well displayed and realistically priced. You know your antiques are just what the men and women in your area need and want for their homes and offices. But how are you going to get the word out about your shop? Certainly, your friends and neighbors know of your new enterprise. You need more than that, though. You can't depend on a sign out front to draw many customers in, either. You need good marketing.

A good marketing plan will spotlight your shop to the community with all the pizzazz of a Hollywood klieg light, then establish you as a knowledgeable and valuable source of information on antiques. A marketing plan can help you determine a reasonable amount of money to allocate to your advertising budget, select the best media for advertising, then evaluate the results of that advertising.

You'll acquire and keep your customers by creating an image for your shop through careful and consistent marketing. What is marketing? Marketing is, plain and simple, promotion. It's just a term that means letting the world know about your shop. For you, as the new owner of an antiques shop, marketing will encompass paid advertising, free public-relations-type publicity, direct mail, networking, and a big grand opening. Your success as a home-based antiques dealer will come from a combination of many forms of promotion, each one reinforcing the power of the other.

Do you need any special training to do all this promotion and advertising? No. By using the information in this chapter, you can easily create and manage your own marketing. No one knows your business as you do, and no one can promote it as well and with as much enthusiasm as you can. You know the antiques business and the type of people who buy antiques. You know your inventory. You understand that this is a cyclical business with high and low months.

The buying and selling of antiques is different from almost any other form of retailing. Above all, it's one where creativity and an eye for value constitute the pillars of success. You'll use these same two attributes in your marketing.

Certainly, you could hire a public relations agency to manage your marketing, but these firms usually work with large companies that have extensive budgets, so their services are quite pricey. Actually, as the owner of your business, you're in a much better position to promote your own shop than any agency professional could. Allocate a few hours every week to doing your own marketing. Once you get into it, you'll probably discover that marketing is actually pleasant and quite creative. (You'll find information on using the Internet for marketing and advertising in Chapter 6.)

Creating Your Marketing Plan

Your first marketing task will be to create a plan to guide you through your promotional efforts for the first year in business. You'll evaluate and adapt this marketing plan, just as you do your business plan, every year. You'll quickly discover that this marketing plan is as important to your business success as is filling your shop with beautiful antiques.

Just as your business plan is a guide to help you think through and resolve the overall conduct of your antiques business, a marketing plan will help you bring customers in and keep them coming back. It's an ongoing process that continues for as long as you remain in business.

Once in place, your marketing plan will act as a road map to guide you, month by month, through both your short-term and your long-term promotion plans. It will help you coordinate your various promotions for the most effective use of your precious dollars. Your plan will spur you to start organizing, well in advance, special events to coincide with holidays and community affairs. You'll always have the money in your budget for a big spring mailing, for example, because you planned for it in January.

The research for your *business* plan results in a great deal of demographic information about your community and the people who patronize other area antiques shops and who will soon become your customers. This information will be invaluable as you plan your marketing schedule. Using these data, write down answers to the following questions:

1. Who is the typical antiques buyer in my town? (Male? Female? What age?)

   _____

2. What is the median family income of this person? _____

   _____

3. What radio station is this person most likely to listen to? _____

   _____

4. What newspaper is this person most likely to read? _____

   _____

5. Roughly, what percentage of my customers will be retired? _____

   _____

6. Will most of my customers live within a thirty-minute drive of my shop? _____

   _____

7. How many tourists visit my town every year? _____

   _____

8. How do most of these tourists travel (car, plane, train)? _____

   _____

9. Where do most of these tourists stay while in town? _____

   _____

10. During which months do most tourists visit here? _____

    _____

Once you've thought through the answers to the preceding questions, you'll have the information you need to plan an effective marketing schedule.

Ready to tackle that marketing plan? Let's break it down into sections, as you did your business plan. (What follows is purely hypothetical. You should adapt these pages to suit your own situation.)

Start off with a few statements that define your annual goals: weekly and monthly media advertising, special promotions, networking plans, image-enhancement plans.

The second section is a month-by-month breakdown of your marketing efforts, based on the answers to your questions listed above and your statements of goals. This section becomes a specific guide for the entire year.

You'll notice that the sample marketing plan for Sally's Antiques (on the following pages) schedules a grand opening celebration, which will probably be the biggest promotion of your first year in business. All the information you need for writing the backgrounder, press releases, and so forth, that are mentioned in this first-year plan begins on page 201.

Your plan should be flexible enough to allow for additions or alterations as the necessity arises. Note that in March and August, Sally markets herself as a speaker at civic clubs. She obviously is successful, because she's actually presenting talks in May and November. The two lines in May and November mentioning the talks are added *after* she receives the go-ahead and the talks are scheduled.

Hint: Buy a large wall calendar that has 2-inch-square blank spaces for each day. Transfer all planned advertising, promotions, contacts, and the like to the appropriate days. You'll then see at a glance what needs to be accomplished on any specific day.

Sample Marketing Plan

Here's how a typical first-year marketing plan for Sally's Antiques might look. Note that this plan begins in March, since March is the month Sally opens her shop. In succeeding years the plan will begin in January. A blank copy of the plan is in the appendix for you to photocopy and use.

Marketing Plan—2005
Sally's Antiques

Goals:

• to hold at least three sales or special events during the year

• to speak to at least two civic groups during the year

• to establish a mailing list of at least 400 past and present customers

• to develop business among summer tourists

Month	Campaign	Budget
March	Weekly ads in *Register.*	4 x $35 = $140
	Call program chairpeople of local civic clubs to offer self as speaker.	
	Call director of City College continuing education program to offer self as seminar leader.	
	Join chamber of commerce.	$125
	Begin plans for May Grand Opening.	
April	Weekly ads in *Register.*	4 x $35 = $140
	Attend Big City Antiques Show.	$5
	Write backgrounder and press releases for Grand Opening.	
	Deliver backgrounder and press releases to editors and program directors.	
	Make preliminary contacts with newspaper editors, radio, and TV program directors for Grand Opening publicity.	
	Prepare talk for City Women's Club.	
	Contact editor of *YourTown City Magazine* about feature story in summer issue.	
	Meet with graphic artist to design flyers for Grand Opening.	$50
	Have flyers printed.	$25
	Distribute flyers.	

Month	Campaign	Budget
May	Weekly ads in *Register,* plus display ad week before Grand Opening.	4 x $35 = $140 1 x $400 = $400
	Ten spots on KABC radio.	$200
	Grand Opening.	
	Buy postcards for Summer Sale.	$100
	Have print shop print cards.	$35
	Run off mailing labels for cards.	$3
	Speak to City Women's Club.	
June	Weekly ads in *Register.*	4 x $35 = $140
	Mail postcards.	
	Make 15% OFF signs.	
July	Weekly ads in *Register.*	4 x $35 = $140
	Summer sale.	
	Begin plans for Pioneer Days promotion.	
	Contact historical society about display for Pioneer Days.	
August	Weekly ads in *Register.*	4 x $35 = $140
	Call program chairpeople of civic clubs again.	
	Write press releases for Pioneer Days promotion.	
	Call *Register* editor about feature for Pioneer Days.	
	Deliver backgrounders and releases to *Register* editor and radio stations.	
	Firm up plans for Pioneer Days with historical society.	
September	Weekly ads in *Register.*	4 x $35 = $140
	Pioneer Days promotion.	

Month	Campaign	Budget
October	Weekly ads in *Register.*	4 x $35 = $140
	Begin plans for Christmas sale.	
	Update mailing list.	
	Buy postcards for Christmas sale.	$60
	Have postcards printed.	$40
	Run off labels for postcards.	$4
November	Weekly ads in *Register.*	4 x $35 = $140
	Prepare talk for Collector's Club.	
	Present talk to Collector's Club.	
	Mail postcards for Christmas sale.	
	Attend Big City Antiques Show.	$5
	Decorate shop.	
December	Weekly ads in *Register.*	4 x $35 = $140
	Hold Christmas Sale.	
	Vacation: Dec. 25–Jan. 8.	

At first glance, all this promotion may seem like a lot of work. After all, you're selling antiques too. By breaking the tasks down into weekly increments, you should be able to handle a similar marketing plan in a few hours a week. Use early mornings, slow hours during the day, or evening hours, whichever suits your schedule and personality best. The reason you have a plan is to help you schedule your time so that you can take advantage of every possible promotional opportunity.

The marketing plan illustrates the two major divisions of marketing. The first, and the one most familiar to many new retailers, is *paid advertising*. It's easy to believe that ads in newspapers, for example, are the best way to publicize a business (and they can be during the first months). In the long run, however, paid advertising is usually less effective than the second type of marketing known as *public relations* or *publicity,* which is free advertising you generate in the local media and through personal contacts.

Paid Advertising

You'll have to include money in your budget for paid advertising. No way around it. Right at first, when all the money's going out and little's coming in, you may well cringe at the thought of paying for advertising. The fact remains that advertising is essential, especially during the first months of business, when your visibility as an antiques shop in the community may be slim indeed. Paid advertising is a guaranteed way to get your name before the public then. Later on, after you've established yourself, you'll be able to garner quite a bit of unpaid promotion. Until then, let's discuss how you can get the most bang for your advertising buck.

It doesn't make sense for the owner of a small home-based antiques shop to use what's termed the shotgun approach to advertising, which means spreading your money and efforts like buckshot over a huge area. This type of advertising works only for very large general-interest firms that appeal to a wide variety of customers—old, young, men, women, low-income, high-income, and so forth. You're better off to use the rifle approach, which is aiming directly at the target. The target is, of course, your customers. This section describes how to use the rifle approach.

Newspaper Advertising

The shotgun approach to newspaper advertising would be to buy ads in a big metropolitan newspaper, one with a circulation of 500,000 or so and read by practically everyone in the entire city. Keep in mind that the vast majority of its readers would be unlikely to become your customers, and your little ads would be lost among the huge department- and discount-store ads. The rifle approach is to buy ads in the local paper that services your small town or in the community paper that is distributed in your section of the big city. Your ads would show up in its less crowded pages, and its readers would live close enough to your shop to be logical customers.

Now let's discuss the two types of paid newspaper advertising: display and classified, otherwise known as the "want ads").

Display Ads. Display ads are the large boxed ones that are scattered throughout the main sections of the paper. They can be highly attractive, especially if they contain graphics, but display ads are also highly expensive—outrageously expensive, in fact. Your grand opening is the one time you should spend the hundreds of dollars to place a display ad in your local paper. For that one-time-only special event, you will get results from such an ad, and it will reinforce the free publicity you get, doubling the impact.

You may have had some training in graphics and layout in one of your business courses. If not, this is one time you should spring for professional help in preparing that all-important grand opening ad. The cost won't be prohibitive, and professionals know how you can get the most value for your advertising dollar. Just be sure your ad follows the tried-and-true format used by every good advertising writer—the AIDA formula.

The figure on the following page is a typical display ad for an antiques shop grand opening. Can you see how this ad uses the AIDA formula? Do you see how this formula works? Does this format seem familiar? Probably so, because you see it every day in ads, brochures, flyers, and other promotional material created by public relations and advertising professionals. You can't go wrong with the AIDA formula in display ads.

The preceding paragraphs described a display ad you might buy for *your own* special

Question: What is the AIDA formula?

Answer: It is a format used by professional advertising people to create professional-quality ads and flyers. Here's how it works:

- The *A* stands for ATTENTION.
- The *I* stands for INTEREST.
- The *D* stands for DESIRE.
- The *A* stands for ACTION.

You'll use the AIDA formula thus: At or near the top of your ad or flyer, you write a headline, some lively text that will attract the reader's *Attention* to the ad by announcing a newsworthy event. You follow the headline with more text that creates *Interest* in your shop or the event. Halfway down you write text that will stimulate the reader's *Desire* to know more about your shop or to attend a special event. Finally, near the end you place some short, punchy text that will motivate the reader to take *Action*, to come into your shop.

promotion. Be wary, however, of spending any advertising money on a display ad that promotes a *community event*, an ad that is simply one of fifty or so other small, similar ads covering an entire page in the paper. You've seen these pages, usually promoting a town's annual event, such as a Chili Cookoff Weekend, Pear Blossom Days, or a Scandinavian Festival.

A representative from your local newspaper may approach you to buy such a display ad, saying it'll be good advertising for you. Frankly, I doubt it. This type of ad is usually a little larger than a business card, and contains scarcely more information than a business card does, yet you have to pay the same high display-ad rate. Unfortunately, these ads just don't carry their weight, especially for a new business.

Classified Ads. The best advice is to forgo display ads except for your grand opening and stick with regular ads in the classified section of the paper, where prices are much more affordable. To be honest, ads for antiques in the classified section are, in most cases, actually more effective than display ads, since many people who are searching for antiques read the classifieds, especially the subsections headed Antiques, Auctions, Furniture, and Garage Sales. Place your own ad in the Antiques category and they can't miss it.

For $30 or $40 a week or less in many smaller newspapers, you can buy a substantial classified ad that will really stand out. Don't hesitate to pay a small additional fee to enclose your classified ad in a strong, decorative border or some other attention-getting device.

The best classified ads are those that highlight a few specific antiques rather than try to catalog a whole laundry list of items. Just be sure the name of your shop is in bold type, along with your address. The following might be a typical classified ad for a home-based antiques shop:

> NEW THIS WEEK AT
> SALLY'S ANTIQUES!
> Fine mahogany sideboard
> Turn-of-the-century rolltop office desk
> 56-piece set of old Noritake china
> Wicker fern stand
> Hundreds of other lovely antiques just
> right for your home or for gifts
> SALLY'S ANTIQUES
> *Where the coffeepot is always on!*
> 123 OAK DRIVE
> 555–6398

Warning: *Never* read your weekly classified ad over the telephone to a clerk at the paper. Always type it and take it in or send it by e-mail. Then insist that it be printed exactly as you wrote it. You don't want to encounter someone with poor spelling and absolutely no knowledge of antiques and end up with an ad that makes you want to scream.

A novice dealer phoned in an ad that mentioned, among several other antiques and collectibles, an Art Deco vanity bench. When she opened her paper two days later, she hit the roof when she saw the vanity bench described as "Art Decoration." She raced to the paper, located the employee who'd taken her ad over the phone, and demanded to know why her ad didn't read as she'd called it in. The employee, who'd never heard the term Art Deco, answered in all innocence, "Well, there was a little space left at the end of the line, and I didn't see any need to abbreviate the word decoration when I could spell it out!"

Consistency is the key to successful classified advertising. Don't place ads a couple of times, then decide they're not paying off. Set up a regular schedule, preferably weekly, and run your ad regardless of any obvious results. Many people will see your ads with the name of your shop the first time or two, and it won't register. But as they read them, week after week, in the same section of the classifieds, they'll begin to notice. Many papers will give you a special rate, too, if you sign a contract for a specified number of insertions. Talk to the advertising manager to receive such a reduced rate.

Radio Advertising

Radio is not usually the best advertising medium for a small antiques shop, but you may want to run a few spots for your grand opening. The rifle approach works at this time, too. Let's assume that the initial research you did for your business plan indicated that your average customer is probably a thirty-nine-year-old married woman with an income of $30,000 per year. Your shop/home is in a suburban community of a large metropolitan city, and this customer lives in that community.

You decide to advertise your grand opening on local radio. Instead of buying time on all three local radio stations, you call each station and ask for the demographics of its listeners. You may discover that one station appeals mostly to teenagers and young adults, and it plays the music they enjoy. Another station plays mostly oldies-but-goodies favored by the over-fifty crowd. The third station plays contemporary jazz and pop. This information tells you to concentrate your radio advertising money with station number three, the one your *average* customer is most likely to listen to.

You'll discover, when talking with the radio's advertising account person, that the station charges a different rate for slots aired at different times of the day. As a rule, the most expensive slots are those aired during what's termed "drive time"—that is, weekdays from 6:00 to 10:00 A.M. and 4:00 to 7:00 P.M. The least expensive slots are often during the middle of the day.

You'll get the most coverage for your money by scheduling those midday slots. Anyone who is at home during the day—retired people, housewives, shift workers—will hear them.

Add to that the many people who listen to radio at work, and you come up with a large portion of the population.

Most advertisements for radio are written to fit into either ten-, thirty-, or sixty-second slots. A ten-second spot consists of approximately twenty words. A thirty-second spot is about sixty words, and a one-minute spot runs around 120 words. You can pack a surprising amount of information into those few words.

The easiest way to write radio spots is to start with a sixty-second one because it allows you the most space to get your message across. Even so, avoid meaningless words. Try to use only those words that carry your message. Once your sixty-second spot is complete, go back and eliminate words until the spot is reduced to thirty, then ten seconds.

Here's a typical sixty-second spot for radio:

> *Sally's Antiques is the newest antiques shop in town, and we're having our big Grand Opening May 17 through 24. Sally's Antiques is the shop in YourTown for primitive furniture, fine nineteenth-century pieces, and those popular collectibles from the turn of the century. At Sally's Antiques you'll find Belleek, Shelley, Limoges, Haviland, and Wedgwood china. We carry reference books on antiques for you serious collectors. Looking for an inexpensive gift? Check out Grandma's Corner in the back room. Nothing there is more than $15. During our Grand Opening we'll have free flowers for the first fifty ladies, and we'll give away two gift certificates worth $25 each. Don't miss it, the big Grand Opening at Sally's Antiques, 123 Oak Drive, where the coffeepot is always on!*

Now let's take that sixty-second spot and delete enough words to bring it down to thirty seconds. Here's what we might come up with:

> *Sally's Antiques, at 123 Oak Drive, is having its big Grand Opening May 17 through 24. Sally's is the shop for primitive furniture, fine nineteenth-century pieces, and turn-of-the-century collectibles, beautiful china and pottery, plus reference books. Register for $25 gift certificates during the big Grand Opening, May 17 through 24, at Sally's Antiques, 123 Oak Drive, where the coffeepot is always on!*

Okay, so your budget is pretty thin and you can only spring for a few ten-second spots. You can still let people know you're in business. Here's how:

Sally's Antiques announces its gala Grand Opening—May 17 through 24. Antiques, collectibles. Register for free gift certificates. Sally's Antiques, 123 Oak Drive.

Amazing, isn't it, the amount of information you can squeeze into twenty short words?

Television Advertising

Forget paid television advertising. It's far too expensive for the average small business. You may be able to get complimentary spots on local television for your special events, however. More about that later.

The Yellow Pages

Everybody "walks their fingers" through the Yellow Pages. It's the fastest, easiest way to locate almost any product or service. A listing in your telephone Yellow Pages can be a top-notch way to draw customers to your shop. In fact, it's undoubtedly the very best way to attract new and out-of-town buyers who don't see your regular newspaper ads.

As a business phone customer, you'll get a complimentary one-line listing in the Yellow Pages. All this includes, however, is the name of your shop, the address, and your phone number.

Unless you're working on an absolute rock-bottom budget, I'd strongly suggest you buy a Yellow Pages display ad. Just like display ads in newspapers, Yellow Pages display ads are outrageously expensive. How about $95 per month for one-sixteenth of a page? (The minimum price depends on the part of the country you live in, the size of your city, and the area covered by the telephone book. An ad in the New York City phone book would cost many times the price of a comparable ad in the phone book for a small town in Wyoming.)

Unlike radio and newspaper ads where you can buy time or space from week to week if you like, you must commit yourself for a full year to Yellow Pages advertising. Nevertheless, many small businesses that seldom advertise elsewhere include money for Yellow Pages ads in their budgets. They're that effective.

Your Yellow Pages ad should follow the AIDA formula mentioned earlier, and this is one time I'd pay a few dollars to have the ad designed by a professional. After all, the ad will be in the book for an entire year, and you can't change it once the type is set. Look in the Yellow Pages under the categories Advertising or Public Relations Counselors for someone to help you compose your ad.

The ad should include the following, in approximately this order:

- the name of your shop in bold, attractive type
- an attention-catching graphic, your logo if you have one
- a listing of the types of antiques you handle
- a mention of any other services you offer (appraisals, estate sales, and so forth)
- encouragement to visit the shop
- your open days and hours
- your telephone number
- your address
- e-mail address and Web site (if you have one)

That's just about all the paid advertising you, as a home-based antiques shop owner, should consider. For more information about Internet Web site advertising, see Chapter 6. Now let's talk about the free promotion you can get for your shop.

Free Advertising: Publicity (Public Relations)

One of the biggest mistakes first-time owners of small businesses make is to depend on paid advertising to promote their shop. Advertising is easy. They just pay their money, get some coverage in the paper, then sit back and consider that they've done all the promotion possible. Uh-uh. There's a whole world of promotion out there just waiting to be tapped for the retailer who's willing to spend time and energy on *publicity*.

Many dealers are totally unaware of the incredible amount of publicity they can get—thousands and thousands of dollars worth—and not pay a dime for it, other than the time and minimal costs necessary to prepare releases.

Free publicity can be in the form of feature stories in newspapers, complete with big photographs of you and your shop. It can be lively spots on radio and even announcements on local television. The antiques business is unique in that antiques dealers can even get other *businesses* to help them promote their own. The beauty of *public relations,* unpaid publicity, is that, according to many surveys, *consumers respond to it three times more often than they do to paid advertising.*

Think about it. Your neighborhood movie theater might run a weekly ad listing the current movies it's showing and call each one "best of the season," "a must see," or "heart-wrenching drama." You've heard and read the same hyperbole so often about so many movies that you seldom pay much attention to it. Yet if you read reviews of the same films, written by a well-respected critic, and the critic highly recommends the films, perhaps using the same words that are in the ads, you'll sit up and pay attention. The implication is that the critic made an unbiased judgment of the movies, whereas the theater would say anything to get us to plunk down our cash for a ticket. The ads are paid advertisement. The reviews are unpaid publicity. See how this works?

The same holds true for you and your shop. People read ads, certainly, and you almost have to run them, but your customers will place more credence in *feature stories* written by a newspaper reporter or editor than they will in the ads. This coverage has the appearance of being a genuine news story. Readers quite naturally feel it is objective and unsolicited, yet you actually are the impetus for the stories.

The information in this chapter will show you how to arrange for newspaper feature stories and community-events-type notices on radio or television. You'll be amazed at the positive responses. You'll generate this free publicity with press releases, backgrounders, public service announcements, and flyers, all of which you can compose yourself.

Press Releases

A press release is a typed page that describes you, your shop, and any special event you plan to hold. Press releases are the accepted method of making contact with the media, and a well-written release will get a busy editor's attention. Most of these editors, however, are overworked, and many have no support staffs, so to get attention a release should follow some pretty specific guidelines. Write your releases using the following format and they're almost guaranteed to be noticed.

Guidelines for a Perfect Press Release

- *Keep the release to one page.* Editors don't have time to read more than that. If they want more information than you can place on one page, they'll ask for it.

- *Place a release date on the first line in the upper-right corner.* If you'd like the release to be printed immediately, type FOR IMMEDIATE RELEASE. Or you can type what's termed an "embargo" by specifying a certain date: RELEASE BETWEEN MAY 8 AND MAY 15, for example. An editor is not obligated, however, to abide by your release date. He will run the story whenever it fits the paper's schedule.

- *Using bold, capital letters, write a one-line headline that accurately describes the subject of the release.* The headline should be catchy and enticing enough to get the editor's attention, but not coy or cute. Just tell it like it is.

- *On the first line of text, write the name of your city and the date you plan to deliver the release.*

- *Double-space all text, and use a plain, easy-to-read typeface.* No script or fancy typefaces, please—editors hate them.

- *Get the five W's of journalism—Who? What? Why? Where? and When?—in the first paragraph or two.* This is the place for your first mention of the event you're promoting.

- *Use simple language, short words, and short sentences when you compose the text, the same type of writing you find in your daily paper.* Editors abhor flowery language and overblown adjectives.

- *Be enthusiastic but objective when describing your shop.* Don't call it the "best antiques shop in the county!" This could be a matter of opinion. "The *newest* antiques shop" or "the only *home-based* antiques shop" is certainly newsworthy, and this is what editors want—news.

- *Get as much solid information as you can on one page.* Remember, the editor probably knows nothing about your shop. You must tweak his curiosity and interest with facts, facts, facts.

- *Include a quotation in the text.* Editors like quotations as they help personalize what might otherwise be a dry story. You'll probably be the source for this quote, so make it lively and quotable.

- *Run your release off on good-quality 8½-by-11-inch paper.* Most of the press releases that land on an editor's desk each morning are printed on stark white paper, so why not print your release on paper with a subtle ivory or gray tint? It'll stand out in that sea of releases and just might get the attention of a harried editor.
- *Place your name and daytime telephone number at the end of the release so that the editor can call you for more information.*
- *Call the paper and ask which editor handles the department that would logically run your release.* That's the person you want to contact.

The figure on page 205 is a typical press release for an antiques shop. With any kind of luck, such a release would result in at least a short news story or mention in a community-events-type column.

Backgrounders

You probably can get much more than short notices in your local paper by including what's called a *backgrounder* with your press release. A backgrounder is one or more typed sheets that give background information about you, your new shop, and any especially interesting or unusual aspects of you and the shop. This is the information the editor will use to determine whether your shop is interesting enough to warrant running a big feature story—and you want that feature story.

A backgrounder includes statistics about you and your shop: shop name, location, your name, and so forth. It also has a quotation from you as the owner and some interesting information that won't fit into the press release. If the editor decides to run a feature about you, the reporter assigned to the story will receive a copy of your backgrounder and will bring it with him to use during the interview. The backgrounder helps the reporter come up with enough questions and information to write the article. The figure on page 206 is a typical backgrounder.

You'll notice in the backgrounder the mention of Sally's extensive collection of majolica pottery. Can you see how such a collection could make an excellent photograph, perhaps with Sally shown holding a particularly valuable piece? Editors are always eager for stories that can be illustrated with photographs.

YOURTOWN'S ONLY HOME-BASED
ANTIQUES SHOP
TO HOLD GRAND OPENING

YourTown, USA, May 5, 2005—Ms. Sally Johnson, owner of Sally's Antiques, announces the Grand Opening of her shop during the week of May 19 through 24. The shop is located at 123 Oak Drive.

Sally's Antiques is the only home-based antiques shop in YourTown. The shop's location, 3 blocks from the Plaza downtown, is within easy walking distance of the main business district, yet it has the atmosphere of a private home. According to Ms. Johnson, "I chose to open my shop in my home because I want to create a homelike atmosphere where my customers can easily visualize any particular antique in their own home."

The first fifty customers to visit the shop during the Grand Opening will receive fresh flowers. There will also be a drawing for two $25 gift certificates, good toward any antique in the shop. The drawing will be held at 5:00 P.M. on the last day of the Grand Opening, May 24. Parking is available on Oak Drive and in the city parking lot on Main Street.

For more information, contact:
Ms. Sally Johnson
(805) 555–6938

Backgrounder

Name of new shop: Sally's Antiques
Location: 123 Oak Drive, YourTown
Telephone number: (805) 555–6938
Owner: Sally Johnson
Hours of operation: 10:00 A.M. to 5:30 P.M., Monday through Saturday

Relevant information:

Sally's Antiques, YourTown's newest antiques shop, is in Sally Johnson's home. This is the only home-based antiques shop in YourTown. Ms. Johnson converted the front three rooms of her home into a 600-square-foot shop that faces Oak Drive. Ms. Johnson will hold a gala Grand Opening celebration of the shop during the week of May 19 to 24.

Ms. Johnson has lived in YourTown for twelve years and has been an avid collector of antiques all her life. Her own collection includes fifty-six pieces of fine majolica pottery, which she acquired in the years she and Mr. Johnson traveled extensively in Europe and this country. Ms. Johnson displays this collection in four glass-fronted cases in the Johnson living quarters, which are now in the rear of the first floor and on the entire upper floor of the family's two-story home.

Ms. Johnson is active in community affairs and is a member of the local Lions club, the Symphony Guild, the Chamber of Commerce, and the YourTown Community Theater group.

She was born in Atlanta, Georgia, and spent her childhood years in a home filled with mid-Victorian antiques. It was then she developed a love for and appreciation of antique furniture and accessories.

According to Ms. Johnson, "Fine antiques are considered one of the best investments today, because, statistically, they increase in value each year. In most cases the construction of antique furniture is superior to that of modern construction methods. In addition, antiques bring beauty into a home and pleasure to their owners. Many people today display a few antiques along with their contemporary furnishings."

The unique aspect of this shop is the area called "Grandma's Corner," which displays moderately priced collectibles, none over $15. No other antiques shop in this area has such an exhibit.

In addition to selling antiques and collectibles, Ms. Johnson appraises antiques in private collections and for insurance purposes. Ms. Johnson also holds estate sales for YourTown residents. These sales are held in the home of the antiques owners and provide an alternative to placing the antiques in auction houses.

When you write your backgrounder, be sure to include anything about you or your shop that would make a good photograph. This information is almost guaranteed to result in some excellent free coverage in your newspaper.

Public Service Announcements (PSAs)

You can use the same press release and backgrounder to generate free public service announcements on local radio to the paid announcements you'll buy. Some radio station program directors will also tape an interview with you and run it many times prior to your grand opening. They use these interviews to fill in spots where their advertising representatives weren't able to sell paid ads. You might be able to get such a tape about your grand opening aired during locally produced home-type shows too.

Some local television stations have what they call "Community Bulletin Boards" or similar programs where they announce community events. You might be able to get some very short announcements about your grand opening on these programs. Don't count on it, though, as most of these announcements concern nonprofit events.

Flyers

Attractive, colorful flyers can be a great way to get the word out about your shop at very little cost. Any copy center can print a flyer, in quantity, on colored paper for about 5 cents a sheet. Assuming that you order 1,000 flyers, your cost will be only $50. (Your costs will decrease to only 3 cents or less per flyer if you order in larger quantities.) With 1,000 flyers in circulation, potentially 1,000 or more people will learn of your shop or of a special promotion. You'd be hard put to reach that many people personally for so little money. Radio ads disappear and can't be recalled the second after they're aired. Newspaper ads must compete with perhaps hundreds of other similar ads, and a newspaper is usually discarded after one reading. A flyer, however, is a highly visible and portable advertisement. A well-composed flyer can contain a wealth of information that simply can't be included in any other type of advertisement.

You could create a flyer that simply gives general information about your shop. This type of flyer is often placed in bed-and-breakfast inns, hotels, chamber of commerce information centers, and other places frequented by tourists. Flyers can be used as direct-mail pieces to announce special promotions. You can also distribute your flyers at antiques shows and flea markets.

Most people will stop to glance over an attractive flyer. Then, if the subject interests them, they'll pick it up and hold it for study later. For all these reasons, I suggest that you consider using flyers to promote your antiques business. Have the flyers run off on 8½-by-11-inch colored stock. Use bold type that's easy to read, and include at least one graphic that is indicative of an antiques shop.

Now take another look at the newspaper display ad (page 196). Do you see that this newspaper display ad for a grand opening could be used just as well for a flyer? The advertising or public relations agency that prepared this ad for Sally Johnson would give her the master copy. She could then take it to a copy center and have as many flyers as she wanted run off to promote her grand opening.

Regardless of who prepares any flyers you might use, just remember the AIDA formula (see page 195), which works equally well in laying out flyers. Get people's *A*ttention with a smashing headline, capture their *I*nterest with compelling text and graphics, instill *D*esire with alluring descriptions, then move them to *A*ction with a forceful suggestion.

Your Grand Opening

Your grand opening is your first and best opportunity to make an impression on the antiques-buying public in your community. Play it for all it's worth!

Publicizing Your Grand Opening

Throughout this chapter you've found examples of typical advertising and public relations devices. All of them can be used in one way or another to promote your grand opening. Ideally, this event should be held for at least a week, beginning on a Friday or Saturday. Don't choose a holiday weekend, though, as most people are too busy having fun on Memorial Day, July Fourth, and Labor Day weekends to generate much enthusiasm for visiting an antiques shop.

Begin your publicity campaign three or four weeks before the actual event. Call every newspaper in your area and ask for the name of the editor who handles local *feature stories*.

The feature-story editor arranges for stories about anything new or interesting happening within the paper's coverage area.

Call each feature-story editor and introduce yourself as the owner of a new shop in town. Explain that you're planning a grand opening that should be a fun event for the community. Ask whether you can bring in a press release and backgrounder for the editor to read. Be enthusiastic! Make your shop sound so interesting that the editor will want to know more about it.

The time of day you make your call is important. Editors frequently work right up to the deadline before a paper goes to press, and they have no time to talk with anyone then. For a morning paper the best time to call is usually early morning. For an afternoon paper the best time is usually early afternoon. Call early in the week for Sunday edition editors.

With any kind of luck, some of these editors will invite you to come in for a preinterview. Arrive all smiles and charm. At this preinterview you must convince the editor or the reporter assigned to talk with you that both you and your new shop are interesting. If you succeed, a time will be set for the formal interview. Leave your press release and backgrounder with the reporter or editor.

The reporter will call you in a few days to set the date for the interview, usually within a week. He will probably want to interview you at your shop, so be sure it is in top-notch shape. At the interview you'll be asked more questions about yourself and your shop. Be sure to give the reporter all the details about your grand opening, and be *enthusiastic*. In all but large cities, the opening of a new shop is genuine news that the paper wants to mention. The paper may assign a photographer to take pictures during the interview, so be well dressed.

Again, I guarantee that any feature story with photographs that results from such an interview will bring in customers.

About two weeks before your grand opening, call all radio stations that cover your area and ask for the person who handles news of community events. This person might be the *news director* or the *program director*. Call this person and, with the same enthusiasm you showed at the newspaper office, briefly describe your new shop and ask whether you can send a press release and backgrounder about your grand opening.

Most newspapers and radio stations won't run a free story about a commercial enterprise if you don't buy an ad occasionally—that's life in the media world. If you've bought some advertising spots for this event, you'll probably get free publicity spots too.

You can try using the same technique to get mentioned on local television. As I noted earlier, however, don't count on it.

You can count on a positive response from colorful flyers, though. Take flyers announcing the grand opening to every hotel, motel, bed-and-breakfast inn, and information center in your area. Ask to have the flyers displayed on a table or counter where people can pick them up. Travelers often have a free hour or two on their hands, and many would like to know of some interesting local place to visit.

Distribute your flyers anywhere that people who might be interested in antiques congregate. Thrift shops, auction houses, flea markets, decorating shops, and so forth are all possibilities. One way to show your gratitude to the owners or managers of these places is by giving them your business card with a notation on it saying "15% discount on one purchase anytime during _____." (Fill in the calendar year for which the discount will apply.) Not only is this a courteous gesture, but it'll bring them into your shop too!

Make sure that all your advertising and publicity mentions some sort of incentive for customers to visit the shop during the grand opening.

Preparing Your Shop for Your Grand Opening

Make your shop as festive as possible for this event. Place bouquets of flowers throughout the shop and on your checkout table (home-grown posies are fine). Have soft, lively music playing on a radio or CD player. Fill pretty bowls with mints and place them on several tables. Decorate potted trees, either outside or inside, with tiny, twinkling white lights. Meet each person who enters the door with a pleasant greeting and an invitation to sign a guest book and register for free gift certificates or any other inducement you're using during the grand opening.

If you have the budget, time, and help, you could also offer punch and cookies to each visitor. Refreshments involve some extra work and expense, though, because you'd have to make the punch, buy the cookies, and rent the punch bowl and dozens of punch cups. I've seen this done at openings, but I'm not at all sure it's worth the effort.

Try to get a relative or friend to help out on the first day or two of the grand opening. Chances are you'll have a crowd, and you, as the shop owner, should be available for pleasant chatting and discussion about your antiques. Your helper can fill in at the checkout table by handling money and wrapping purchases.

Media Coverage After Your Grand Opening

You can get additional after-the-event media coverage by calling newspapers to announce winners of the gift certificates. This would be genuine news in a small town. Even a brief mention in the paper will be worth far more in publicity than the value of the certificates. You might also take a photograph of the drawing and the people who win the certificates and offer the photograph to the paper.

You'll derive additional value from your gift certificates because the people who register for them have to sign slips of paper with their name, address, and telephone number. These slips provide you with an instant mailing list.

Think how often you've seen the same type of device used by large companies. You sign up for a chance at a free trip to Hawaii, a new car, or some other prize, and pretty soon you're receiving promotional mail or phone calls asking you to buy life insurance, aluminum siding, cemetery plots, vacuum cleaners, or whatever. In your case you'd use this list, along with the names in the guest book, later to send announcements of sales or some other promotional event. It's a perfectly legitimate marketing strategy.

Follow-up Publicity

The fallout from the media blitz surrounding your grand opening will last for several weeks. After that you'll want to continue your publicity campaign to hold on to present customers and gain new ones. Some of the ways you can accomplish this feat are through direct mail, welcome services, special events, speaking engagements, public service, and networking.

Direct Mail

Direct mail is any correspondence you send your customers through the mail. For an antiques shop this usually means postcards and flyers. Direct mailings are certainly not inexpensive at today's postage rates, but they're one sure way to keep in touch with your customers, let them know you value their patronage, and at the same time inform them of special events at your shop.

You might consider getting a bulk mailing permit if you plan to mail hundreds of letters several times a year. At this writing the permit costs $150 annually and allows you to mail a letter-size envelope for 26.8 cents. Each mailing must consist of at least 200 envelopes. You can print the required postage onto the envelope with a postage meter or glue special stamps individually on the envelopes. For an additional one-time-only fee of $150, you can get another permit that allows you to have bulk-rate postage preprinted on your envelopes. This last method is a real time-saver and bypasses both the postage meter and the stamps.

You can't get any special rate for postcards, however. No matter how many postcards you send, you must stick on those 23-cent stamps or purchase them with postage affixed for 25 cents.

Suppose your mailing list is still in its infancy and you're not ready to go the bulk-mail route. Here's another suggestion. Did you know that you can get envelopes preprinted with your shop's name and return address *and* prestamped for little more than the cost of the stamp itself? Can you guess where? Surprise! It's nowhere other than the good old United States Postal Service.

To order these envelopes, go to your local Post Office and fill out a "Personalized Envelope Order" form. (The form is reproduced on the following page.) You'll include on the form your shop name and return address. You may even include a couple of lines of advertising if you like. At the time this book is being written, charges for the envelopes are as follows:

- long regular envelope: $205 for a box of 500
- long window envelope: $205 for a box of 500
- short regular envelope: $202 for a box of 500
- short window envelope: $202 for a box of 500

In about four weeks the envelopes will arrive in the mail. Each envelope, regardless of type, will carry a preprinted stamp in the upper-right corner and your shop name and return address in the upper-left corner. A little calculation will show you that you pay about 4 cents each, above the cost of the postage, for these preprinted envelopes. This is a real bargain, when you consider what printers charge to print envelopes with your shop's name and return address.

United States Postal Service
Personalized Envelope Order Form

DO NOT STAPLE OR ATTACH CLIPS

Boxes of 500

Description	Size	Denom-ination	Item No.	No. Boxes	x Price per Box	= Cost
Ribbon Star Regular	6 ¾"	37 ¢	2641		$202.00	$
Ribbon Star Regular	10"	37 ¢	2141		$205.00	
Ribbon Star Window	6 ¾"	37 ¢	2642		$202.00	
Ribbon Star Window	10"	37 ¢	2142		$205.00	
Ribbon Star Security (Regular)	9"	37 ¢	2143		$205.00	
Ribbon Star Security (Window)	9"	37 ¢	2154		$205.00	
Non-profit Sheep* (Regular)	6 ¾"	5 ¢	2627		$ 42.00	
Non-profit Sheep* (Regular)	10"	5 ¢	2151		$ 45.00	
Non-profit Sheep* (Window)	6 ¾"	5 ¢	2628		$ 42.00	
Non-profit Sheep* (Window)	10"	5 ¢	2152		$ 45.00	
Eagle, Standard Mail*	10"	10 ¢	2153		$ 70.00	

* Must Meet Postal Requirements for This Category

Printing of Upper Left-Hand Return-Only Address *(Not Addressee)*

Daytime Telephone
(   )

Ship to Address *(If different from above)*. Must Include Full Name and Address.

Shipping & Handling Charge *(Max. charge $9.85 for each address printed)*	
One Box	$5.85
Two or More Boxes	9.85

Subtotal	$
Shipping & Handling	
TOTAL Boxes of 500	$

Boxes of 50

Description	Size	Denom-ination	Item No.	No. Boxes	x Price Per Box	= Cost
Ribbon Star Regular	6 ¾"	37 ¢	2625		$22.00	$
Ribbon Star Regular	10"	37 ¢	2105		$22.00	
Ribbon Star Window	6 ¾"	37 ¢	2626		$22.00	
Ribbon Star Window	10"	37 ¢	2106		$22.00	
Ribbon Star Security (Regular)	9"	37 ¢	2108		$22.00	
Ribbon Star Security (Window)	9"	37 ¢	2109		$22.00	

Printing of Upper Left-Hand Return-Only Address *(Not Addressee)*

Daytime Telephone
(   )

Ship to Address *(If different from above)*. Must Include Full Name and Address.

Subtotal	$
Shipping & Handling	
TOTAL Boxes of 50	$

Amount of Order	Charge
$.00 to 22.00	$3.85
22.01 - 44.00	4.85
44.01 - 66.00	5.85
66.01 - 88.00	6.85
88.01 - 110.00	7.85
$110.01 - 132.00	8.85
132.01 and up	9.85

*** NOTE: Insufficent payment will result in either reduced quantites shipped, or your order not processed. ***

Total Enclosed and Method of Payment

Make check or money order **(do not send cash)** payable to
US Postal Service
and mail to:
STAMP FULFILLMENT SERVICES
US POSTAL SERVICE
PO BOX 7247
PHILADELPHIA PA 19170-7103

or:

TOTAL Boxes of 500	$
TOTAL Boxes of 50	
Shipping & Handling Fee	
GRAND TOTAL	$

NOTE: Other designs will be available at a later date.

Charge to my: ☐ Discover ☐ VISA ☐ MasterCard ☐ American Express ☐ Diner's Club

Mo.   Yr.

Credit Card No. [   ]

Exp. Date:

Signature _____

☐ I authorize the Postal Service to adjust credit card payment if necessary

PS Form **3203-X,** June 2002

This form available at www.usps.gov.com

Welcome Services

You may know your local welcome service by the name of Welcome Wagon, Western Welcome, or any of a half-dozen other names. All of them, though, provide essentially the same service. Friendly residents call on newcomers to town, bringing along a basket full of gifts, samples, and discount coupons that can be redeemed at local firms. Signing on with a welcome service is a superb way to let new residents know of your shop. Many times people moving to a new community know little or nothing about the town. They have few if any friends. They're eager to begin meeting people and learning what the business community has to offer.

As an antiques dealer, you'd probably want to offer these newcomers a discount on their first purchase at your shop. Everyone loves a bargain, and these people are almost sure to stop in to take advantage of your offer. They are prime candidates to become your customers. After all, they're all furnishing and decorating new homes.

Here's how a welcome service works. You pay the welcome service company a fee and provide the representatives with a supply of cards describing your shop and mentioning the discount. In most communities the welcome service is listed in the Yellow Pages. If you can't find one there, call your local chamber of commerce.

Special Events

Your grand opening was probably your first special event. Plan on others throughout the year too. If you make these events unique, you'll probably generate some free publicity in the local media.

Every business owner is a constant target for donations from dozens of perfectly worthwhile charities and benefits. And like most other people, you probably have a hard time refusing anyone. It seems heartless to turn down an eager youth collecting money to send his debating team to a conference or a hardworking volunteer soliciting for the Heart or Lung Foundation. Yet the owner of a new business can hardly afford to parcel out scarce funds for anything but maintaining the business.

Make a substantial contribution each year to your favorite charity. Turn down practically all requests for money from others. Answer when they ask: "Thanks for coming by, but I give all my charitable money to _____ [whatever charity you support]." No one has ever questioned that answer.

Here are some suggestions for special events:

- Hold a contest in your shop one weekend when people come in dressed in antique or period-style clothing. Take photographs of each entrant, then award a prize or gift certificate for the most authentic in three categories: men, women, and children. A museum curator could be the judge. Call the newspaper and request a reporter and photographer to be on hand when the prizes are awarded.
- If your town has an annual history-based event such as Pioneers' Day, Gold Rush Festival, or Revolutionary War Reenactment, have a special sale to coincide with the dates. Wear a period costume in the shop on those days.
- Make a deal with the town historian to be in your shop for two or three hours one weekend to tell stories about the town's beginnings. Request a reporter and photographer from the newspaper to cover the event.
- Plan a special display of historic artifacts or memorabilia belonging to local residents. Again, alert the media.

You get the drift. Create events that are newsworthy. You'll gain many customers every time your shop is featured in the newspaper, and longtime customers will continue to look upon your shop as being the most interesting in town. They'll tell their friends, who will then become customers.

Speaking Engagements

You may not look upon yourself as a public speaker, but I'll bet you've spent many an hour talking about antiques with friends. Right? You discuss trends, restoration tips, building a collection, authenticating an antique, and so forth. You can take this natural interest in discussing antiques with friends one step further: Turn it into public speaking, which will quickly give you high visibility in your community.

The program directors of church groups, special-interest clubs, and service clubs are always looking for speakers who can give twenty- or thirty-minute talks at club meetings. As the owner of an antiques shop, you're an accepted authority on the subject, so volunteer your services.

Once you're scheduled to talk, ask what the main focus of the club is, then tailor your talk to fit. You might talk about the history of sundials for a garden club. An investment club would be interested in learning how antiques rise in value and how trends affect prices. Members attending an AARP (American Association of Retired Persons) meeting might like to know how to determine the value of antiques they own.

Perhaps you'll receive an invitation to give a thirty-minute talk at the monthly luncheon of the local retired teachers' group. Though the program chairman who called may leave the topic up to you, ask if club members are especially interested in a particular category of antiques, such as Victorian china and glass. Then put together an informal talk on the history and characteristics of various kinds of antique china and cut glass. Since everyone responds well to the "show and tell" technique, take along several examples to illustrate your points. The talk will be entertaining and informative, and it should give the listeners interesting facts about antiques that will add to their pleasure in collecting them.

Question: How can I evaluate the effectiveness of my advertising and publicity efforts?

Answer: You can do so in several ways:
- Ask every new customer, "How did you hear about my shop?"
- Place a coupon on your flyers that entitles the recipient to a small gift (perhaps a bag of your potpourri) or a 10 percent discount on a purchase if the coupon is redeemed before a certain date. The number of coupons redeemed is a good indication of the number of people who responded to the flyer.
- Watch your daily records closely to see whether sales increase substantially on days following those when your ads appear.
- Examine your records following a special in-house event to see whether sales increase substantially.

Now, as a businessperson, always try to find a way to make such a talk pay off in sales. So, take a stack of gift certificates that offer the bearers 15 percent off any antique in the shop. Give each person at the luncheon one of these certificates. You'll sell many antiques as a result, and with any kind of luck, the people who redeem the certificates will become loyal customers!

Short talks such as these are easy to present. You're simply talking about something you know very well. You'll hardly ever get paid for giving these talks—a complimentary lunch is usually the extent of remuneration. Statistically, though, many of the people hearing you will visit your shop, perhaps for the first time. Another big plus is that your name will be printed in the paper as the speaker for that meeting—free publicity!

If you find that you enjoy public speaking, you might want to consider presenting workshops through a college's continuing education department. Look over continuing education catalogs and you'll find dozens of fascinating courses offered, all geared toward making life more pleasant or interesting for the participants. Presenting these workshops does involve more time and preparation than the short talks. However, you will actually get paid for giving them. Generally, classes run from one and a half to two hours. The fee is usually $20 to $35 per hour no matter how many students, so tell the school to limit your enrollment to fifteen to twenty-five students. If you have more than that, you'll not have enough time to answer questions.

Public Service

Most dealers feel they should give something back to the community in which they live. As an antiques dealer—and therefore an expert on the subject—you can use your knowledge in many ways. Your time would be welcomed at the local history museum in identifying period furniture and accessories. Perhaps you could help catalog and display rare books in your public library. You could sponsor a student from a high school business class and act as a mentor in showing him the ropes of running a business.

Let the local amateur theater group know you'll lend pieces from your shop to be used as props in its plays. Not only will you earn the group's undying gratitude, but your shop will be acknowledged in the program. Again, free *publicity!*

Networking

Make time for contacts that can result in a great deal of profitable business. Get to know the real estate agents in town and leave some of your business cards in their offices. Half of their clients are buying homes, and they may need furniture and accessories to decorate them.

Join clubs and organizations and attend their meetings. Volunteer to work on committees. You'll quickly develop friends who may become good customers.

Question: How can I compete with other antiques shops in my town? They already have a loyal following and I'm the new kid on the block, so to speak.

Answer: You can do it in several ways.

- Make yourself and your shop highly visible to the community through constant networking.

- Stay open a half hour in the afternoon after your competition has closed its doors. If the shops in town close at 5:00 P.M., you stay open until 5:30. If they close at 5:30 P.M., keep your doors open until 6:00. Many people browse in one antiques shop after another for hours before deciding to buy. If your shop is still open after the others are closed, you might very well garner that last-minute business.

- Make a special effort to draw interior decorators to your shop. These professionals often work with well-to-do clients who allow them free rein in choosing items for their homes. In most cases the decorators don't quibble about prices. You might stay open one night a month for interior decorators and serve a little wine and cheese to help them relax after a busy day. Show any unusual or decorative antiques you've acquired since the last open house. Find out what antiques they need to decorate their clients' homes and try to locate those pieces. Call a decorator if something comes in that you know she can sell to a client. Working with interior decorators is a win-win situation for everyone. You sell the antiques at top dollar, the decorators get a commission on the sale from their clients, and the clients receive lovely antiques for their homes.

Chapter Ten

Other Ways to Make Money in Antiques

Your home-based shop will be your primary source of income as an antiques dealer, especially during your first year in business. Later on, though, as you acquire a reputation as an expert in the field, you may want to branch out into one or more other antiques-related fields. Many antiques dealers do just that, which adds substantial amounts to their annual incomes.

Some of the related businesses you might consider are selling at antiques shows, appraising antiques, managing estate sales, selling high-ticket antiques by appointment only, and subleasing space to another entrepreneur.

Selling at Antiques Shows

Among dealers the practice of selling at antiques shows is called "working the shows." You'll hear that phrase constantly as you network with other antiques dealers. "Working the shows" means renting space at an antiques show and selling some of your merchandise for two or more days from that space.

Some dealers work only the shows in their own towns. Others work any show within a few hours' driving time. A few dealers set up annual itineraries, usually in summer, that take them around a circuit of a half-dozen or more shows.

Whether it's one show or ten, this is by far the best way to present the greatest number of antiques to the greatest number of potential customers in the least amount of time. Instead of waiting for buyers to come to your shop, you take your merchandise to them. Lovers of antiques flock to these shows because they know they can see more antiques in two or three hours than they would in days of trudging from one shop to another. As a result, at each show thousands of transactions take place between buyers and dealers.

Some annual shows are sponsored by nonprofit organizations such as symphony guilds or large service clubs. These groups look upon the proceeds from space rental and entrance fees at the shows as one of their primary sources of income. Other antiques shows are strictly commercial affairs, managed by professional organizers. All proceeds from space rental and entrance fees become the property of the promoters. As a rule, there's little difference in the types of shows as long as the sponsors know their business and manage the shows in a professional manner.

A popular variation of the seasonal show is one held regularly and frequently at the same site. One promoter has been successfully managing such antiques shows for years. He advertises each show extensively in the local media, and the ads draw thousands of browsers and buyers.

This promoter rents a huge armory building for the third Sunday of each month. Dealers sign up in advance for the 3-by-8-foot tables he provides, paying him $12 for each table they reserve. Most dealers rent at least two or three tables. They cover the admittedly ugly tables with cloths and display their china, glassware, jewelry, and so forth on portable shelves.

The procedure for working the shows is pretty much the same, whether you exhibit at annual, semiannual, or monthly affairs. How would you, as a home-based antiques dealer, begin working the shows? Start by making an objective assessment of every show you can attend.

1. *Attend as many shows as possible throughout your state or section of the country.* Your local newspaper will run announcements of antiques shows in your immediate area. Read the various antiques trade papers, such as *AntiqueWeek* and *Maine Antique Digest,* for dates and locations of these shows. No matter where you live—in the East or West, North or South—you'll find similar regional pub-

lications that describe area antiques shows. Pay entrance fees ranging from $2.00 to $10.00 and you'll be exposed to hours and hours of firsthand education about how antiques shows are run, how dealers manage their booths, and what they're selling.

2. *Observe the preshow promotions.* Do they appear to be professional and well coordinated? Is the newspaper advertising backed up with spots on radio and local television? Do you find flyers announcing the shows at local antiques shops? Is the hall where the show will be held attractive and in an easily accessible location? Does the hall have plenty of free parking?

3. *Once a show opens, take an hour or so to observe the way it operates.* Is it clean and well lighted? (Buyers want to examine an antique in strong light before purchasing it.) Do the people in charge appear to be cheerful and well organized? (Frazzled promoters are invariably poorly organized.) Are the aisles wide enough for customers to walk freely from one booth to another? (People don't like to be jammed, shoulder to shoulder, in a public building.) Did the promoters provide some kind of food service for customers, and does the food appear appetizing? (People will linger at a show much longer if they can refresh themselves with a soft drink and snack.) Are the antiques on display of a high quality? (You can't charge reasonable prices for antiques at a show that has a flea-market ambience.) All these factors contribute to an antiques show that will attract buyers.

4. *Check out the dealers themselves.* Happy dealers indicate well-managed shows. Approach a few of the dealers at a show and explain that you're thinking of reserving space in the next show. Don't be shy. Most dealers in antiques love to talk about their profession, and they'll be glad to chat with you. Ask them what they think of the show. Has their relationship with the organizers been pleasant? Do they feel the space rental is reasonable? Most important, ask these dealers *if they plan to rent space at the next show run by this particular group or promoter.* Dealers don't return to a show if they don't make money the first time.

5. *Check out what people are buying.* Is furniture a big seller? What about cut glass and china? Are the dealers who display jewelry and sterling silver doing a brisk business? Or do customers seem more interested in moderately priced col-

lectibles? Or does it seem that there's little pattern to what customers are buying and that almost any well-priced antique will sell? The answers to these questions will help you decide what to bring to the show yourself.

6. *Observe which areas attract the most customers.* You may notice that some areas of the hall draw more customers than other areas. As a rule, knowledgeable dealers like to be close to the hall's entrance, since customers tend to start their shopping there. Most people then gravitate to the right, so spaces on the right side of the entrance are usually more desirable than those on the left. Spaces in corners can be dark, and many people will avoid them. Dealers in balcony spaces often report lower sales volume because some people won't or can't walk up steps.

If you're satisfied with the operation of a show, scout around until you find the promoter. Introduce yourself and say that you'd like to reserve a space in the next show. Don't be surprised if you hear that the show—a year away—is already fully reserved. This isn't uncommon with some of the better shows in large cities. If the show is full, just ask to have your name put on a waiting list. I've found that, many times, a few dealers have to cancel their reservations and the promoters then rent their spaces to others. Once you're accepted for the show, you'll be asked to sign a contract. Most promoters will ask for one-half the booth fee at the time you sign the contract, with the balance due on the first day of the show.

One home-based dealer who works several large shows each year has this advice for the first-timer: "Start small! Contract for a small booth, maybe 10 by 10 feet. That way you'll have a chance to learn the ropes with minimal expense." She did just that at her first show and now feels quite confident renting triple that space in shows all over her area.

Some promoters charge a fee for space but don't include a table in the fee. Many of them, however, will rent tables to dealers for the duration of a show, usually charging $8 to $12 per table per day. Obviously, you'd need several tables for even a small booth, and since most shows run at least three days, you can see that table rental at this type of show could be a major expense. Most knowledgeable dealers construct their own tables. A sheet of plywood with galvanized-pipe legs that can be screwed into sockets in minutes makes a dandy table. Of course, you must cover the raw plywood with attractive fabric. The easiest solution is to buy king-size sheets and adapt them to fit the tables. Your initial expense will be about the same as renting tables for just one day, and you'll own the tables for every subsequent show.

You'll also need attractive shelves to display your antiques. Serviceable shelves can be made from painted shelving or plate glass. The choice is yours. Just look at what other dealers use at shows and decide what would work for you.

Finally, even though the hall appears to be well lighted, you should provide additional lamps to spotlight your antiques. One dealer didn't realize how dull and uninviting his booth was until he got it set up, then looked around at some of the booths nearby. All the other dealers had high-intensity spots beaming on the crystal and china. Their booths looked sparkling and bright, and his looked dreary. So he bought a half-dozen spots at the nearest discount store. It made all the difference in the world!

As we all know, every new venture takes longer to complete than planned, and setting up your booth at an antiques show is no exception. You'll need hours to unload your van or truck, unpack boxes, and arrange the antiques attractively. Show promoters understand this, so, assuming a show opens on Friday morning, they allow dealers to enter the hall on Thursday afternoon to set up their booths. Then, even though you might feel on Thursday night that your booth is ready for the first customers, always arrive early on Friday morning to dust the furniture again and perhaps rearrange a few things.

During the run of the show, continue to rearrange both your furniture and your smaller antiques. Many people return to a show again and again on subsequent days, walking up and down the same aisles before they decide to buy. They may pass right by a pretty whatnot displayed on one side of your booth, then finally see it on the other side of the booth on their third visit.

Be careful about filling cabinets with smaller items, especially if the cabinet is also for sale. Buyers will tend to pass by a full cabinet thinking it's just a prop. If you have any type of cabinet for sale, make sure it's prominently featured.

As your antiques sell, you'll also want to rearrange your stock so that your shelves appear full. Customers like to feel they have a good selection to choose from. They're far more likely to buy if you seem to have an ample supply of antiques, even during the last few hours of the show.

Many dealers tuck a box or two of extra stock underneath their tables. When the shelves begin to look a little bare, they just dip into these reserves and, presto, a brand-new look. You may be thinking, "Well, why not put all that extra stock out right at first?" The answer is that you don't want your shelves to look too crowded. Statistically, you'll sell more antiques if the shelves appear orderly and attractive, not jumbled up as at a flea market.

You'll notice that some dealers bring folding chairs to sit on. This isn't a very good idea. Granted, you'll get tired standing, but psychologically, customers feel that a dealer who's sitting is uninterested. Also, it's a great temptation to chat with other dealers and neglect potential customers if you're seated. To forestall fatigue, bring high-energy snacks such as granola bars, nuts, or trail mix to munch on discreetly between customers. Arrange for a friend, spouse, or fellow dealer to watch the booth for you occasionally. You can then sit for a few minutes and eat a nutritious lunch at the snack bar, take midmorning and midafternoon breaks, and visit the restroom. Some shows even provide hostesses who'll fill in for you in this respect.

Most shows run for at least two and sometimes three or four days. This time affords you an opportunity, assuming you live close by, to adjust your stock. You may find on the first day of the show, for example, that you sell a great deal of furniture but comparatively little glassware. As a result, you know to dismantle one of the tables holding glassware and fill the space with furniture you'll bring from the shop the next morning. The watchword here is *flexibility*. Display what people want to buy and you'll make money.

A real side benefit to working the shows is that you're subtly advertising the existence of your shop. Be sure to have posted somewhere in the booth an attractive sign that mentions the name and location of your shop. Many people will visit you at the shop even if they don't buy during the show. Most dealers also place business cards in little trays somewhere in the booth. Encourage everyone who comes into the booth to take a card.

Do you adjust your prices to compensate for your costs in exhibiting at the shows? No. Most dealers who work the shows build show costs into their prices. No customer wants to discover a different price on an antique in a show from the price she saw on the same piece in your shop, and vice versa. This is not good merchandising.

Are there any disadvantages to working the shows? Of course. You must pack your antiques and haul them in either a van or a truck to the show site. Then you have to pack up and haul back to the shop anything that doesn't sell. Most show promoters, however, provide muscles in the form of big teenage boys to help exhibitors unload and load their antiques. If you need such help, be sure to arrange for it with the promoter in advance.

Another disadvantage of working the shows is that you have to be there for a show's duration. If you work alone in your shop, you must either close it during the show or hire someone to work in your place. You'll also have to stay in hotels or motels if a show is more than an hour's drive from your home. Many shows don't close until 8:00 or 9:00 in the evening, and driving any distance after a full day of selling can be a real drag, especially when you have to get up early and drive back to the show the next day.

On the whole, most dealers in antiques find working the shows both profitable and fun. I recommend that you give it a try.

Appraising Antiques

Many people need to have their antiques appraised for one reason or another, and you'll be asked many times to perform this service.

In all likelihood you won't qualify as a *licensed appraiser*. To become certified with the American Society of Appraisers as an antiques appraiser, you must go through a rigid application process and be employed full-time as an appraiser. Many dealers, however, perform *informal appraisals* for their customers. This is perfectly legal as long as you don't advertise yourself as a certified appraiser or claim to be one.

The main criterion of an informal appraiser is to have a working knowledge of antiques. Certainly, you don't have to possess the expertise of an appraiser at Sotheby's, but you should be able to recognize specific styles in antiques and be able to locate and reference their current values. Two incidents show how you might use your abilities as an antiques dealer to enhance your income.

A young woman came to a reputable dealer, needing an informal appraisal of an antique rocking chair that had been lost by a moving company. The moving company actually wanted to depreciate its value because it was used. She had three photographs of the chair, so the dealer could easily determine its style and relative age. She also told him the year she had bought the chair and how much she'd paid for it. All this information gave him something to go on. Then he checked the current prices of similar rocking chairs in local antiques shops. Once the dealer had this information, he began preparing a folder that he could present to the moving company. He took the photographs to a copy center and had them laser-printed onto one sheet and also photocopied a page from a book whose text said that antiques increase in value each year. Then he typed a report in which he gave his estimate of the antique's current value and listed his own credentials as a dealer in antiques.

The dealer enclosed all this in a card-stock cover and gave it to the young woman, along with his invoice. The invoice covered the copy center charges and a reasonable fee for the dealer's time spent in researching the value of the rocking chair. Even though this was an informal appraisal, the moving company accepted it and paid the woman for the lost rocking chair.

On another occasion, a woman who had inherited a portion of her mother's considerable estate, including a houseful of antiques of every vintage, approached this same dealer. She needed an inventory of the antiques with their values for tax purposes. The dealer visited her home and made notes about every antique. He also took a photograph of each piece with his 35mm camera. After having the film developed at a one-hour photo drop, he reviewed his notes, using the pictures as guides. Because many of the antiques were quite old—seventeenth-century German and English—he didn't want to rely on his own judgment about them, so he reinforced his basic knowledge with information from several current price guides and came up with an approximate value for each piece. The dealer created an inventory that listed the antiques, their description, and his appraisal of their value. The woman was delighted with this service, especially when he handed her the photographs. She hadn't expected to receive them. They'll be invaluable to her in case of fire or theft of any antique in the collection.

Certified appraisers charge exceptionally high rates for their services—up to $150 per hour plus expenses. Most antiques dealers aren't in that rarefied category and must be realistic about how to invoice for informal appraising. Some dealers base their charges on the hourly rate interior decorators receive for their services. But before doing any informal appraising, you need to check who will accept informal appraisals. It pays to research this before you do an appraisal for someone and she finds out later she can't use it.

Managing Estate Sales

One of the fastest ways to make the most money in antiques is by selling someone else's property at an estate sale. Although these sales involve a great deal of work on your part, none of your own money is invested other than for advertising or temporary help. You invest your time and energy only, and you receive a commission of 30 percent—the usual fee—on everything you sell.

How do you get started as an estate seller? First, have the words *Estate Sales* printed on your business cards. Place a sign to that effect somewhere in your shop. Mention the service below your address in every newspaper classified ad you run. List it in your Yellow Pages ad. It won't be long before the phone starts ringing with people eager for you to dispose of their belongings for them. Sometimes they'll be the children of an elderly parent who has died or moved into a rest home. Many times your calls will come from people who are retiring, moving into a condominium, and weeding out a lifetime of possessions that won't fit into a smaller home.

Once you've firmed up the dates with a client, you're ready to advertise the sale. In your local newspaper place a display ad that lists some of the most interesting items, antique and otherwise, and schedule the ad to run about one week prior to the sale. List all the interesting antiques on postcards and send the cards to everyone on your mailing list, again, about one week before the sale. This is the method used by everyone who handles estate sales. The newspaper ad will bring in buyers of both antiques and nonantiques, whereas the postcards will alert your regular customers to the antiques in the sale.

Obviously, to justify the expense of this advertising, any sale must consist of hundreds of items. You may, on occasion, be approached by a seller who has only a half or third as much as you need to make a sale worthwhile. There's one way to take advantage of such an offer, assuming you have a large storage space available. You simply move the merchandise to your storage space, hold it until your next scheduled sale, and combine the two. Such a procedure means physically moving many pieces of furniture and boxes from the owner's home to your storage space, then moving them again to the sale venue. This is a lot of work. Frankly, the owners would have to agree to a much larger commission before you'd pledge yourself to such an arrangement.

Don't even think about managing an estate sale alone. You need help before, during, and after the event. Otherwise, you'll be a candidate for the loony bin by midafternoon on the first day of the sale. Once you have possession of your client's home, you and your helper must sort through, organize, and price every piece the owners leave behind—every pillowcase, every pot, every box of Christmas ornaments, every pair of gloves, every potted plant, and so forth. You may have to wash a mountain of glasses and dishes too.

You'll nearly always hold estate sales on weekends in your clients' homes. Many of these homes are quite small, so experienced estate sales managers often use a take-a-number system to avoid a bone-crushing, wall-to-wall mob during the first minutes of a sale. As customers arrive—usually long before the published time to open—they're given a number that identifies their place in line—first come, first served. Depending on the size of the home, the manager may allow fifteen or twenty people in at a time. Within a half hour this first crush is usually over, and she can open the door to any and all comers.

In most cases the owners of the homes must vacate them at least three or four days prior to the sale, as you need that much time to sort, clean, and price the merchandise. Once, a friend went to an estate sale where, at the very moment buyers were crowding in the front door, the owners were rushing out the back, leaving their breakfast plates, covered with bits of egg and toast, on the kitchen table. You can avoid this disaster by having a written agreement with your clients that spells out all the particulars of the sale.

All the miscellaneous household stuff you have to deal with will bring in plenty of money if you price it just a little higher than you would for a yard sale. The real money-makers, however, will be the antiques and collectibles. You'll be swamped with both dealers and collectors at any sale where you advertise antiques. Dealers will, in fact, become your most loyal customers at estate sales. As dealers, they have to buy at prices that will enable them to add a decent markup and make a profit, so you have to price the antiques in the sale accordingly. You'll be most successful if you price antiques and collectibles at about one-third their retail values.

Why one-third of retail? Then, you'll probably say, you'd buy the most desirable antiques yourself. Yes, unless the owner specifically forbids it, you certainly can buy antiques from the sale before the door opens, but you have to be honest. Price every piece as though it were being offered to the public, then pay that price yourself. At one-third retail you'll still get a good deal. In addition, you'll also collect the commission on that sale, which is, in effect, giving you a 30 percent discount over the already low price.

Just as you use psychology when displaying antiques in your shop by putting the most popular and salable items at eye level, you'll use psychology in your estate sales by placing antiques and collectibles in the first rooms that customers enter. Normally, these will be the living and dining rooms. Display china, crystal, pottery, silver, dolls, and any other especially collectible antiques on tables where customers can see and examine the pieces quickly, and position furniture wherever it will be seen most easily. Serious buyers, including dealers, never waste a moment at estate sales. They expect to sail through the home at record speed in the hope of beating others to the choice antiques. Casual buyers, on the other hand, may spend an hour or more wandering from room to room through the home.

They expect to look over every single item in their search for bargains. As a result, you can use a back bedroom to stack ordinary linens, put ordinary kitchenware in the kitchen, and put tools, outdoor furniture, and such, in the garage or the backyard.

Station your helper at a card table near the front door to act as cashier. This will free you to roam through the home, answering questions and assisting customers. Both of you should keep a sharp eye out for shoplifters. Unfortunately, this type of petty thievery does happen at estate sales.

The owners may leave some very valuable antiques with you—fine jewelry, jade figurines, complete sets of china, and the like. In all honesty, you have to ticket these pieces with high prices. Often, no one will be willing to pay those prices, yet you need to sell the antiques. The solution some estate sales managers use is to put an "Offer Box" at the cashier's table. Any customer may place a bid in the box for any item. The box is opened at a specified time, and if the items have not sold before that, they are awarded to the people making the highest bids.

Most estate sales managers mark anything left at closing on the first day of the sale down to half-price for the second day. Then, during the last hour or so before closing, it's often "Make me an offer!" time. They'll do almost anything to move the last items out. Whatever is left at closing is usually boxed and taken to the Salvation Army or Goodwill for a tax credit. The owner gets that credit, of course.

Your final task is to tally all sales and write the owner a check for 70 percent of the amount. Then put your feet up and relax. You've earned your 30 percent!

Selling High-Ticket Antiques by Appointment Only

Appointment-only selling is a minor aspect of dealing in antiques but one that you may want to consider now or sometime in the future. In this case dealers don't maintain traditional shops with display shelves and such. They don't have signs out front inviting any and all to come in and browse. These dealers work only with serious collectors who are in the market for high-ticket antiques.

Clients of an appointment-only antiques dealer phone and make an appointment to visit the dealer's home. This meeting may have all the ambience of a visit between two old friends who simply sit down and enjoy a cup of tea served in antique china.

Other Ways to Make Money in Antiques

Appointment-only antiques dealers get most of their business through word-of-mouth referrals from satisfied customers. A few place discreet advertisements in decorating magazines that simply mention their services, not specific antiques. Some appointment-only dealers work with interior decorators who constantly search for unusual or rare antiques for their clients.

Many appointment-only dealers buy nothing in advance for resale. They work with their clients to determine the ideal antique for a certain location in the client's home, then set out to locate a piece to fill that need. These dealers spread the word through the antiques dealers' network that they're searching for that piece. They may haunt auctions or fine antiques galleries in their quest. Once they find the desired item, they purchase it, usually with the understanding that it can be returned if the client refuses it, and have it delivered to her homes. The client examines the piece and, if it's satisfactory, buys it. The dealer, of course, adds a substantial profit into the final price.

Other appointment-only dealers buy fine antiques without a *specific* client in mind, but, like any traditional dealer, assume that their considerable investment will eventually pay off. Since this is an extremely low-key business, some of these dealers mingle the antiques they plan to sell with their own family pieces, literally making the entire home a shop. When a pair of French chairs, a Sheraton dining table, an early-nineteenth-century sleigh bed, or a sterling silver candelabra sells, the dealer simply replaces it with another antique. In the meantime the original piece has been a part of the home decor. These antiques dealers often make extensive buying trips to Europe, New York, New Orleans, or other centers to select their stock.

Some of these dealers set aside a portion of their home strictly for their merchandise, but those areas never resemble a traditional antiques shop. They actually suggest a fine home, complete with lovely furniture and accessories. The feeling is always one of elegance and gentility.

Appointment-only selling requires an extensive knowledge of and experience in working with fine antiques. The location must be one where a considerable portion of the population has the means to invest in expensive furnishings. The dealer's home should be as tasteful as that of her clients. Sales and turnover may be exceedingly slow in comparison to those in the traditional shop, but the financial rewards can be great for the successful appointment-only dealer.

Subleasing Space to Another Entrepreneur

Do you have, or can you create, space in your home to be used by another business? Not another antiques shop, but perhaps a secondhand bookstore, or a fine crafts shop? Granted, such an arrangement would be impossible for many home-based antiques dealers. Nevertheless, for anyone with a large home and minimal personal requirements, subleasing space can be an excellent way to create extra income. Depending on the amount of extra space available, you could easily derive several hundred dollars a month in rents.

Naturally, any business you admit into your home would have to be compatible with antiques. Properly chosen, however, such an endeavor can actually *produce* business for your antiques shop, especially if there's easy indoor access from one shop into the other.

Let's visualize a scenario. Four friends browse through a bookstore searching for first editions. While they chat, they can't help but see displayed in the next room dozens of equally lovely antiques in your shop. What would be more natural than to drift over there and take a look?

The same scenario could hold true for almost any shop whose personality is harmonious with that of antiques. The owner of such a home-based antiques shop could even place some of her pieces in the adjacent shop to be sold on commission. A bookshop could place a small church pew along a wall for the comfort of browsers. A crafts shop might display some of its prettiest goodies on a series of small tables. Each of these antiques would be for sale, and the owner of the bookstore or other business would receive a nice commission on any sale—a win-win situation for everyone. Persons who sublease space get the use of attractive antiques, and the owner of the antiques shop has an additional outlet for her merchandise.

A Final Word

There are no magic roads to success in this or any other business. Hard work, enthusiasm, and persistence can accomplish miracles. Calvin Coolidge's quote (on the right) says it all.

Press On

Nothing in the world can take the place of persistence. Talent will not; nothing is more common than unsuccessful men with talent. Genius will not; unrewarded genius is almost a proverb. Education will not; the world is full of educated derelicts. Persistence and determination alone are omnipotent.

Appendix

Government Publications

Small Business Administration

The following titles are available for download from the SBA Web site (www.sba.gov) in PDF format for Adobe Acrobat Reader (available for free download from www.adobe.com.).

Business Plan for Home-Based Business— #MP15
Planning and Goal Setting for Small Business— #MP6
How to Buy or Sell a Business— #MP16
Problems in Managing a Family-Owned Business— #MP3
Checklist for Going Into Business— #MP12
Computerizing Your Business— #MP14
Advertising— #MT11
Marketing Strategies for Growing Businesses— #EB2
Marketing Plan Workbook (09/97)
ABCs of Borrowing— #FM1
Understanding Cash Flow— #FM4

Internal Revenue Service

The following instruction forms are available for download from the Internal Revenue Service Web site (www.irs.gov) in PDF format for Adobe Acrobat Reader.

Business Use of a Car— #917
Business Use of Your Home— #587
Depreciation— #534
Miscellaneous Deductions— #529
Recordkeeping for a Small Business— #552, #583
Self-Employment Tax— #533
Tax Guide for Small Business— #334
Tax Information for Direct Sellers— #911
Taxpayers Starting a Business— #583
Travel, Entertainment, and Gift Expenses— #463

Small Business Development Centers

You can find a Small Business Development Center close to your home, no matter where you live. Locate the nearest office through the Internet at www.sba.gov/hotlist/sbdc.html. This Web site provides links to all the centers in your state.

Antiques Price Guides

(These guides are issued annually with updated information.)

Antique Trader's Antiques and Collectibles Price Guide, Krause Publications, WI
Flea Market Trader, Collector Books, Paducah, KY
Garage Sale & Flea Market Annual, Collector Books, Paducah, KY
Kovels' Antiques & Collectibles Price List, Crown Books, NY
The Official Price Guide to Antiques and Collectibles, House of Collectibles, NY
Pictorial Price Guide to American Antiques, Penquin Putnam, NY
Schroeder's, Collector Books, Paducah, KY
Wallace-Homestead Price Guide to American Country Antiques,
    Wallace-Homestead Book Company, Radnor, PA
Warman's Antiques and Collectibles Price Guide, Wallace-Homestead Book
    Company, Radnor, PA

Antiques Reference Books

Following are just a few of the dozens of titles available, and many are updated regularly. Check your local library for other books on specific antiques.

The Bulfinch Anatomy of Antique Furniture, Bulfinch Press, MA
Garden Antiques and Collectibles, Friedman/Fairfax Publishing, NY
Lyle Official Antiques Review, Berkley Publishing Group, NY

From Schiffer Publishing, Atglen, PA:
American Bisque, Mary Jane Glacomini
Antique Wicker, Heywood-Wakefield Catalog
Cowgirls: Early Images and Collectibles, Judy Crandall
Fun Buttons, Peggy Ann Osbourne
Gas Station Collectibles, Mitch Stenzler

Indian Baskets, Sarah Turnbaugh and William A. Turnbaugh
Miniature Perfume Bottles, Glinda Bowman
Rhinestones!, Nancy Schiffer

From Collector Books, Paducah, KY:
Antique Tins, Fred Dodge
Blue Ridge Dinnerware, Betty Newbound
Carnival Glass, Bill Edwards
Collectible Aluminum Identification and Price Guide, Everett Grist
Elegant Glassware of the Depression Era, Gene Florence
Fishing Lure Collectibles, Dudley Murphy with Rick Edmister
Fostoria Stemware, Milbra Long and Emily Seate
Goldstein's Coca-Cola Collectibles, Sheldon Goldstein and Helen Goldstein
Hall China, Margaret Whitmyer
Lefton China, Loretta Delozier
Made in Japan Ceramics Identification & Values, Carole White
Milk Glass, Betty Newbound
Radios, Marty Bunis with Sue Bunis
Schroeder's Collectible Toys, Sharon Huxford and Bob Huxford

From Wallace-Homestead Book Company, Radnor, PA:
Hake's Guide to Advertising Collectibles, Theodore L. Hake
Warman's English & Continental Pottery & Porcelain, Susan D. Bagdade and Allen D. Bagdade

From Hobby House Press, Grantsville, MD:
Blue Book of Dolls and Values, Jan Foulke
Teddy Bear & Friends, Helen Sieverling

From Avon Books, NY:
Collectible Magazines Identification and Price Guide, David K. Henkel

From Prize Publishing, Medford, OR:
Carnival Chalk Prizes I and II, Thomas Morris

From Shadow Enterprises, Cedar, MN:
Silhouette Collectibles on Glass, Shirley Mace

The two largest publishers of antiques reference books will send catalogs of their current publications to dealers. Request catalogs from Schiffer Publishing Company, 77 Lower Valley Road, Atglen, PA 19310, and Schroeder Publishing Inc., P.O. Box 3009, Paducah, KY 42002–3009.

Cash Flow Projections

	Jan.	Feb.	Mar.	Apr.	May	
1. Beginning Cash Balance						
2. Cash Receipts						
a. Cash sales						
b. Estate sales						
c. Appraisals						
d. Consignments						
e. Other						
3. Total Cash Receipts						
4. Cash Disbursements						
a. Merchandise						
b. Accounting						
c. Advertising						
d. Auto expense						
e. Contributions						
f. Delivery expenses						
g. Electricity						
h. Heat						
i. Insurance						
j. Laundry						
k. Legal expenses						
l. Miscellaneous expenses						
m. Office expenses						
n. Postage						
o. Rent/mortgage						
p. Repairs						
q. Telephone						
r. Dues/subscriptions						
s. Travel expenses						
t. Estimated tax payments						
u. Owner withdrawal						
5. Net Cash Flow						
6. Ending Cash Balance						

	June	July	Aug.	Sept.	Oct.	Nov.	Dec.

Detail of Monthly Expenditures

MDSE AND MATERIALS PAID BY CASH AND CHECKS

DAY	TO WHOM PAID	CHECK NO.	AMOUNT

OTHER EXPENDITURES BY CHECKS AND CASH

DAY	TO WHOM PAID	CHECK NO.	ACCT. NO.	AMOUNT

Carried Forward												

Carried Forward												

Continuation Sheet

MDSE AND MATERIALS PAID BY CASH AND CHECKS

DAY	TO WHOM PAID	CHECK NO.	AMOUNT	

OTHER EXPENDITURES BY CHECKS AND CASH

DAY	TO WHOM PAID	CHECK NO.	ACCT. NO.	AMOUNT	

Carried Forward

Carried Forward

Chart of Accounts

EXPENDITURES

ACCT NO.	ACCOUNT	TOTAL THIS MONTH	TOTAL UP TO THIS MONTH	TOTAL TO DATE
	DEDUCTIBLE			
1	MDSE. - MATERIALS			
2	ACCOUNTING			
3	ADVERTISING			
4	AUTO EXPENSE			
5	CARTONS, ETC.			
6	CONTRIBUTIONS			
7	DELIVERY EXP.			
8	ELECTRICITY			
9	ENTERTAINMENT			
10	FREIGHT AND EXPR.			
11	HEAT			
12	INSURANCE			
13	INTEREST			
14	LAUNDRY			
15	LEGAL EXPENSE			
16	LICENSES			
17	MISC. EXP.			
18	OFFICE EXP.			
19	POSTAGE			
20	RENT			

TOTAL RECEIPTS FROM BUSINESS OR PROFESSION

DAY	AMOUNT		
1			
2			
3			
4			
5			
6			
7			
8			
9			
10			
11			
12			
13			
14			
15			
16			
17			
18			
19			

21	REPAIRS
22	TAX-SALES
23	TAX-SOC. SEC./MED.
24	TAX-STATE U.I.
25	TAX-OTHER
26	SELLING EXP.
27	SUPPLIES
28	TELEPHONE
29	TRADE DUES, ETC.
30	TRAVELING EXP.
31	WAGES AND COMM.
32	WATER
	SUB-TOTAL
	NON-DEDUCTIBLE
51	NOTES PAYABLE
52	FEDERAL INC. TAX
53	LOANS PAYABLE
54	LOANS RECEIVABLE
55	PERSONAL
56	FIXED ASSETS

TOTAL THIS MONTH

TOTAL UP TO THIS MONTH

TOTAL TO DATE

TOTAL THIS MONTH

TOTAL UP TO THIS MONTH

TOTAL TO DATE

Sample File

Code	Item	Cost	Price	Sold At	Date	% Markup

Marketing Plan

Date: _____

Goals for this year:

1. _____
2. _____
3. _____
4. _____

Goals for second year:

1. _____
2. _____

Goals for fifth year:

1. _____
2. _____

Month	Campaign	Budget
January		
February		
March		

Month	Campaign	Budget
April		
May		
June		
July		
August		
September		
October		
November		
December		

Markdown Inventory

Code #	Item	Purchase Price	Original Price	Sale Price

Index

About the Author

The late Jacquelyn Peake was a popular author of eleven how-to books, including *How to Recognize and Refinish Antiques for Pleasure and Profit,* also published by The Globe Pequot Press. Ms. Peake lived in Whitefish, Montana, in a house full of antiques that she had collected for years.

About the Editor

As an avid collector of a variety of antiques and collectibles for the last twenty years, Bob Brooke knows what he's writing about. Besides writing about antiques, Brooke conducts seminars on antiques for various organizations, including the Smithsonian Institution in Washington, D.C. In addition, he has also sold in flea markets and shops. His antiques articles have appeared in many antiques and consumer publications, including *British Heritage, AntiqueWeek, American Antiquities, Southeastern Antiquing and Collecting Magazine, History Magazine,* and many others. To read more of his articles, visit his main Web site, Writing at Its Best (www.bobbrooke.com) or his specialty antiques site, the Antiques Almanac (www.theantiquesalmanac.com).

TIME FOR A CHANGE?

If you're interested in becoming your own boss, changing careers, earning extra cash, or just adding some excitement to your life, this informative series provides the tools you need to launch and maintain a successful home business. Each book is filled with insider information from professionals in the know, and includes:

- Advice on how to attract first-time customers, maintain a loyal client base, and price services competitively and profitably

- Details on start-up costs and zoning regulations

- Helpful, easy-to-use worksheets and questionnaires

- Listings of trade contacts and organizations

"I highly recommend reading [this] series. . . . All of these works delve into marketing, financial management, and just about anything you would need to know to take the plunge in a new venture."

—Steve Rubel, *Mac Home Journal*

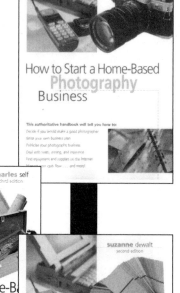